THE
GREAT SALMON
BEATS

DAVID & CHARLES' FIELDSPORTS AND FISHING TITLES

THE GREAT SALMON BEATS

Crawford Little

DAVID & CHARLES
Newton Abbot   London

To Jamie and David

My sons, great friends and fishing companions,
who make me very proud

British Library Cataloguing in Publication Data
Little, Crawford
   The great salmon beats.
   1. Great Britain. Salmon & trout. Angling
   I. Title
   799.1'755

   ISBN 0-7153-9296-4

Typeset by Typesetters (Birmingham) Ltd
Smethwick, West Midlands
and printed in Great Britain
by Butler & Tanner Ltd, Frome and London
for David & Charles Publishers plc
Brunel House   Newton Abbot   Devon

CONTENTS

FOREWORD

In setting out to write this book, I made a firm resolve that it should not be a gazette of who catches what, where, when and for how much. What I have been striving to achieve is to create a broad picture of salmon fishing, beats and rivers in the closing years of the twentieth century, but set within their historical context.

In choosing rivers and beats for inclusion my thoughts have not been too heavily affected by catch figures. If it were otherwise, I should have hardly included the Dart and yet left out my own native Nith, on whose banks I live, and which produced a rod and line catch in excess of 4,000 salmon and grilse last season. Instead, I have tried to single out individual names for specific illustrative purposes. The classic rivers obviously merit inclusion for all sorts of reasons – others might not be so obvious, but I hope their inclusion can be justified. The Thurso provides good sport but more importantly, for my purpose in this book, is a virtually unique example of a significant salmon river in its entirety, from source to sea, has been managed by one family throughout the development of salmon harvesting techniques and social and economic change. Equally, the present Lord Thurso's attitude to the continuing role of netting is at variance with most modern, rod and line thinking on the subject. Then there is the Helmsdale, a fantastic river, and one which is an outstanding example of co-operation between proprietors. The Awe is now but a shadow of the great river that it once was, and the reason is not hard to find. The character of the Kirkaig is virtually unique, the Laxford remains almost entirely preserved, and the Grimersta is the jewel in the crown of Hebridean salmon river and loch systems – it also provides employment in a remote rural economy.

And so it goes on. The Conon has experienced the full range of modern market and economic forces. Time and again it has been the subject of heated political debates; it has been hydroised and time shared and still it soldiers on . . . Arthur Oglesby has stated that his own long term view is that time sharing has to be just about the worst thing that can happen to a salmon river. To an extent, I would echo his sentiment, certainly where fishing weeks are sold in perpetuity, leading to widely shared ownership and very real uncertainties as to longer term management. This, of course, is a very different case from the more benevolent situation where an estate may choose to sell off, say, the next seven, ten or twenty-one years' fishing rights by the week, whereby they raise a useful capital sum and their tenants secure their fishing for a fixed term, with the fishing then reverted to the estate which remains responsible for management throughout the entire period. Then there is the Beauly, where the basic concept of fisheries management – to enhance productivity and limit alternative forms of harvest and predation – has been applied so successfully, and, because of this, a four-figure number of fishermen are able to enjoy what can be excellent sport each season.

The traditional scene on most great salmon beats has changed, and continues to change, dramatically. Some things are for the better – the sport is now open to a far wider section of the community. Other things are regrettable or downright bad. I was talking to a keen fisherman of the older generation only yesterday, who said to me: 'You know, Crawford, things have changed so much in my lifetime. Today, there is so much money and these get-rich-quick entrepreneurs chasing shooting and fishing that I just don't know where it is all going to end. And there is still so much apathy toward the commercial exploitation on the one hand, and political and environmental indifference on the other, that goodness knows where it is all going to end. What sort of salmon fishing will there be for your sons and my grandsons?'

There are many who will echo these thoughts. It is not just the older generation who have witnessed these changes. I am still only in my mid-thirties but have, luckily, fished for salmon through the last quarter century. And yet, despite all the negative things that we have witnessed, there is another side to the coin. Nobody, twenty-five years ago, even in their wildest fantasies would have predicted the Tyne emerging as the most productive salmon river in England.

Bearing that in mind, we can put many of the modern worries about salmon fishing into some sort of context. True, we are now faced with a situation that could be described as too many people chasing too few fish and fishing but, now that we have so many more people involved in the sport, we should be able to bring increased pressure to enhance existing fisheries as well as bring other rivers back into productivity.

What I hope may emerge from this book is that the management and enhancement of salmon fishing, on great beats and elsewhere, may be difficult to achieve, but remains simple in concept. As I said of the Beauly, we must enhance the productivity of the river and salmon resource at the same time as striving to limit alternative harvest to rod and line. Other rivers show us what can be achieved through the close co-operation of proprietors. And, very sadly, there are more than enough examples of what can happen to once great beats and rivers when the needs of the fishery and fish are not placed high enough on the list of considerations.

And so, as we move into the closing decade of this century, it seems a good time to be taking stock of what we may have lost, what we still hold, and what we might gain. Remember the words of the late King George VI: 'The wildlife of today is not ours to dispose of as we please. We have it in trust. We must account for it to those who come after.'

It is with that thought in mind that I dedicate this book to my young sons and, indeed, to all the younger generation of fishermen who may inherit so much or so little. Only we can decide which.

CHAPTER 1

SALMON RIVERS AND BEATS

In the summer months, when even the highest pastures cry out for rain, the mountain streams and burns that feed the river shrink to a gurgling trickle of champagne over golden sands, shingle and rock. In the crystal-clear water, trout and young salmon can be seen, gently finning and waiting for food, darting for shelter beneath the overhanging banks and behind rocks at the merest hint of danger.

In autumn, when mature salmon that have been returning to the river from the sea finally penetrate to these headwaters, this quiet scene is transformed. Grilse and salmon will not have come this far up the river to the furthermost spawning areas until the rains have transformed them into cascading torrents of black, peat-stained water and cream-coloured foam. The salmon that have come this far are no longer the gleaming hard-flanked and high-backed fish that once delighted the fisherman. They lost the inclination or ability to feed when they entered the river. Now, their thin, emaciated bodies, their flanks encased in a thick tartan skin of harsh red, purple, brown and gold, are a pathetic testament to the fish they once were.

The ritual of mating over, the spent fish, kelts as they are called, will summon the last vestiges of their energy to make the final, desperate retreat to the sea. Few of them will survive. The staring eyes of a kelt as it makes a last attempt to stay on an even keel before finally being swept away into some back eddy may seem to signal defeat. But there is only victory in having lived its life, faced the dangers, and overcome the heavy odds that are stacked against it. With its partner, it has played its significant part in ensuring the survival of its species. In a thousand streams of hundreds more rivers, couples of Atlantic salmon have savoured their ultimate task.

Generations upon generations of salmon have experienced this cycle of life from death. It might seem an unchanging existence in a constant landscape. Certainly, the soul of the river seems immortal. Forests may come and go and man may alter the very character of the river with his dams, hydro-electric schemes, abstraction, impounding and pollution, but he seldom destroys the river entirely. Nature is patient, and the river will still be there. The danger is that the salmon may be exploited or, more likely, callously ignored into destruction.

Salmon and rivers; rivers and salmon. To me, the two are inseparable. Simply being on the banks of a salmon river gives me profound pleasure. An astrologer might say that this is because I was born a piscean. I know little of such things. What I do know is the recognition of kindred feelings with Roderick Haig Brown when, in his book *A River Never Sleeps*, he closed with the words: 'Perhaps fishing is, for me, only an excuse to be near rivers. If so, I'm glad I thought of it.'

In the modern age, it is no longer sufficient simply to love and enjoy rivers. We must understand them as well. That way, we see how easy it is for man to upset nature's delicate balance. Only then can we protect them, the salmon, and the sporting inheritance of the great salmon beats.

Many of the problems facing salmon rivers and beats, as with so many problems in our ever shrinking world, lie in the fact that more and more people are chasing what is, in some cases, a diminishing supply.

The number of salmon fishermen increases each year. The fishing scene has changed drastically since the time when proprietors considered their rivers and beats as virtually unworthy of valuation. As short a time ago as the 1930s, the left bank of the lower Oykel, from mid-July to the end of September, was thrown in free with the sporting lease for grouse shooting and stag stalking. It is not easy to find out how many salmon were taken in those days of 'part-time fishers', but today one would expect to catch 200 salmon from that stretch at that time of the season. And they threw it in for free! The reason, in fact, was simple. There just weren't enough fishermen to take all the beats.

Since World War II, there has been an explosion in demand for salmon fishing. Whatever may be said about the redistribution of wealth, increased leisure time and the mass ownership of cars, the result is more and more fishermen flocking north, and the numbers seeking access to prime salmon beats increase with each passing season.

The new generation of fishermen, however, is not so wealthy as to be able to fish like the 'sporting gentlemen of old'. Today, most salmon fishermen think in terms of sharing a beat with friends for a week. Some will manage a fortnight. Contrast this with the turn of the century and before when a not insignificant proportion of sporting tenants would lease the whole of a sporting estate – shooting, fishing and stalking – for the entire season or certainly for months rather than weeks.

Dugald Macintyre in his book *Memories of a Highland Gamekeeper* gives an interesting account of the organisation and planning involved when a family and their friends moved north for the fishing. His employer, in the following description, was Mr G. F. McCorquodale.

I was delighted when my employer asked me to visit him at his fine fishing water on the Spey. He rented thirteen miles of the river Spey when he lived in Tulchan Lodge . . . There were thirteen boats on Mr McCorquodale's part of the Spey. When we had finished with one side of a pool we crossed by boat and fished the other side . . .

Mr McCorquodale had hired a special train for his family and servants, and another 'special' carrying coal arrived at Advie Station the following week. King George V's doings were all the talk of the Lodge people of course; for he had been staying at Tulchan on the previous grouse shooting season.

A kelt being returned to the river. With their flesh emaciated after long months of fasting and their last reserves of energy used up in mating, these spent fish fall back to the sea. Few of them survive

Fisherman and fish – the satisfaction of success with salmon. Demand for salmon fishing far outpaces supply in the modern age

A salmon jumping the falls at Rosehall on the Cassley. The salmon's migration is one of the most fascinating aspects of our natural world

Dugald Macintyre also gives us an insight into the life of gillies and keepers of the day, very different from the often solitary existence of single-handed men of today.

Life at the Lodge was quite enjoyable for me. There was young Frank Grant, a grand piper and violin player, and Williams, the head gillie, who could gaff running salmon in deep water far better and more surely than either Frank Grant or I; and John Cruickshank's cottage was close at hand . . .

A surprising number of the old men of Speyside had been soldiers in their youth. They had seen service in the Seaforths, or Camerons, or Black Watch, and their old stories were worth hearing . . .

Mr McCorquodale gave fortnightly dances to his servants and tenants. All in the district had in fact a free invitation to attend the dances.

I met numerous natives of Speyside at those dances, where gamekeepers and gillies provided the music from their pipes. The pipers were sons of fathers who had fought Britain's battles abroad. You could hear tales of the Relief of Lucknow, the taking of Quebec, and of the Battle of Balaclava from the lips of the old soldiers who had participated in the battles, or from their sons.

Incidentally, Mr McCorquodale was described by Macintyre as about the best of the many good salmon anglers he had watched at work. Little wonder in that. G. F. McCorquodale caught 10,000 salmon in his lifetime, over 8,000 in the Spey alone. He caught eight salmon before his breakfast one fine morning. But to return to the present day . . .

Nowadays, a beat that once saw one or two fishermen in a week is now let to half-a-dozen. They will perhaps share one gillie between them, in contrast with a time when one gillie for one gentleman was standard practice. Equally, sharing one rod between two fishermen is becoming a common practice. It can be said to be done for companionship but fishery managers must beware lest it be a ruse to disguise the water being flogged from dawn to dusk, the partners acting in relay. Of course, it has to be admitted that some proprietors and their managers or agents are quite happy for this sort of thing to be done in the expectation that, by possibly increasing the catch, the letting and capital value of the beat will be enhanced.

Time-share is another recent innovation. It was initially received with great acclaim in many quarters, particularly by those who had endured long waiting lists to get onto prime waters, waiting for existing tenants to retire or expire, and who had the cheque books and bank balances to prove that he who pays the piper calls the tune. However, many people are now asking whether short-term profits for the sporting entrepreneurs involved justify the long-term uncertainties over management. Some time-share beats are obviously in capable hands; others may not be. Let us not name names.

Rod-shares, time-shares, weekly lets or whatever, the accent in modern salmon fishing throughout the British Isles is on hustle and bustle and catching fish – as many fish as possible in the short time available to the modern fisherman.

Gillies on the great and not-so-great salmon beats are well aware of this. On one side, they may have a proprietor or agent pushing to ensure that capital and rental

A fisherman and his dogs, alone in beautiful surroundings. Who will join with us in the fight to conserve and enhance salmon stocks?

values are enhanced or at least maintained. And then there are the guests who are more demanding than ever. Men who pay a small fortune to fish for salmon expect to get value for money, which many can only equate with the number of salmon caught. Some are quick to show their displeasure if things do not go according to plan. This is one of the gillie's great complaints: 'Help them to catch one salmon and they want another. When they have caught two salmon, they want twenty. And then thirty . . . There is no pleasing some of them. They are no better than the netsmen and fishmongers.' Certainly in the world of salmon fishing there are those who seem to have forgotten that fishing is meant to be for fun and enjoyment. It is to be hoped that the majority are still able to accept the simple pleasures of being beside a great river and can still regard the fish they catch as a bonus – a red-letter day, as something to be savoured rather than expected.

However men decide to conduct their sport, one thing is certain, and it has been said already. In the future, it will not be sufficient simply to maintain salmon stocks on the great rivers and beats. We should, for the sake of the salmon as well as ourselves, be seeking to increase and enhance the stocks. This might not seem to be such an optimistic note to strike at the present time. After all, there is some hope in the fact that nowadays things are not nearly so bad as they were in the late sixties when the scourge of UDN (Ulcerative Dermal Neucrosis) was at its height, coupled with the then uncontrolled massacre and general mayhem being inflicted on salmon stocks at their ocean feeding grounds. Even so, we cannot afford to become complacent. What we are witnessing, even with the buying-off and suspension of so many estuary and coastal nets, may be no more than a transitory, short-term upswing to be seen against the background of a more general downswing in the fortunes of salmon.

Today, most of the problems likely to be encountered by salmon are environmental or arising out of the commercial exploitation of the water resource or its surroundings. Who will help fishermen to guard salmon stocks? The Salmon Bill of recent times, while offering some small rays of hope, is considered by many to be little more than a 'paper tiger'. Will the popular conservation movements, steadily gaining in public support, take up the cause?

My own view is that the salmon themselves, as an individual species, can expect little recognition from this quarter. However, as a species dependent on the condition of their environment, which we can at least hope will be better managed in the future, they may benefit a great deal.

Popular conservation bodies are dependent upon public subscription and support for their policies and actions. Unfortunately, for most of the urban-based public, it is not enough for conservation to be done, it must be seen to be done. Nature has become a 'hands-on' affair. People want to see it, feel it and hear it. Safari parks and carefully tended nature trails allow the public to come and gawp at wild nature concentrated into a contrived situation. You can motivate public opinion by media coverage of the fate of pandas or gorillas. They can see and respond to them. But what about salmon? The damned things are always underwater! How would you get

Joe Public and his wife to invest in the future of wet and slimy when they want warm and furry?

If you argue that popular conservation movements have prompted the saving of the whale and are now turning their attention to the dolphin, you miss the point; these are intelligent mammals and not fish. We all grow up with a strange fascination and sense of awe of the whales, but nobody has yet made a TV series and written songs about 'Flipper the Salmon'. And you have to think of it another way. What support would the whalers have got if they had asked the public to fight and spend to save and encourage whale populations simply so that they, the whalers, could kill more of them?

What the public do care and know about, however, is water. They drink it, bathe in it and put it to a hundred other uses. They would like to think that the water in their taps, and in their lakes, rivers and streams, is clean and pure. People are genuinely concerned about acid rain, even if they are fairly vague as to its cause and effect. They no longer accept that rivers can be suppliers of fresh clean water and collectors of household and commercial effluent at one and the same time. Industrial polluters are seen as social enemies. It is understood that the management of water has a profound effect on the environment as a whole. Nobody wants to walk and picnic with their children on the banks of an open sewer.

Government, industry and society in general are starting to clean up their acts in regard to the water resource. And this must be good not only for the protection but also the enhancement of salmon stocks.

Some 25 years ago, I was standing on the bridge of a ship with my father and uncle. The vessel was in for a refit at a Sunderland dockyard. I looked down into the River Wear and could hardly believe my eyes. The tide had just turned and the oily waters of the ebb carried a suspension of human effluent. Swimming steadily against this, just beneath the surface, was a salmon. I called to the others. Yes, indeed it was a salmon. Smiles quickly faded to sombre looks. 'It will not last an hour in that filth.'

Twenty-five years on, the Wear has been cleaned up out of all recognition. The runs of salmon and sea trout into the river may not be massive, but the club at Bishop Auckland reported 72 salmon and sea trout in September 1987. That is more than simply a good start. Neighbouring Tyne has now emerged as the most prolific salmon river in England.

Just as important as the change in fortunes on the Wear is the case of the Clyde. Not so many years ago, nobody would have imagined that salmon would be running the river through the centre of Glasgow and past the shipyards.

It may seem strange to discuss rivers such as the Tyne, Wear and the Clyde in a book dedicated to 'The Great Salmon Beats'. But here is clear evidence of the benefits to the salmon fishing scene wherever, not so much by design but as a peripheral benefit from the wishes of environmentally conscious people.

What we gain on the swings of conservation, however, we tend to lose on the roundabouts. Proprietors, their agents and those who fish the great salmon beats have in the past been strong in calling for both the increased culling of seals and the removal of some of the protection afforded to birds that prey on immature salmon. Whatever their case may be, they really cannot expect much sympathy. The seal has practically become the figurehead of the popular British conservation movement, particularly since its populations have suffered so dramatically from disease. When the seals recover, as they surely will, we must accept that the purely recreational needs of those who choose to 'kill for sport' can hardly be expected to merit consideration and a sympathetic hearing against the needs of a natural predator – particularly one which appeals so strongly to the public imagination.

On acid rain, which has severely affected the productivity of a number of salmon rivers, the Government surely cannot drag its heels for much longer. The technology is there to control emissions. It is now up to intent and investment. In the meantime, one suggestion for a cure to some of the effects of acid rain on rivers and fish stocks has been a resumption of the subsidies for liming on upland farms. This ignores the fact that subsidies and grants are dirty words now in the corridors of power that rule the Common Agricultural Policy in Brussels. Farmers are now faced with the prospect of free trade and quotas, rather than encouragement for production. The situation on the uplands where the sources of our great rivers are to be found is that farming is facing severe problems. Any reversal in the declining fortunes of grouse will have come too late for those thousands of acres of moor which, in the decade and more when they could show no income, disappeared under the forester's plough, to become some small part of the investment portfolio of an absentee landowner, super-sport, disc-jockey or the like.

Upland forestry is, for a number of reasons, something that can have a severe effect on a river's productivity and how well, or badly, it fishes. Some beats have suffered. But they and others have suffered just as badly from water impounding and abstraction, coastal and estuary netting, massive and carefully organised poaching, the destruction of spawning redds and a dozen other things. What these activities all have in common, other than their adverse effect on fish and fishing, is that they are expensive and difficult to oppose. At the end of the day, the future of the great salmon beats, and salmon fishing with rod and line in general, will depend entirely upon how much commitment and capital can be found to protect them.

The statisticians can tell us how much money, how many hundreds of pounds, we spend as individuals to catch one salmon. They can tell us how many millions upon millions we spend collectively on sporting rents and rates, hotel bills, travel, endless bits and pieces of tackle and so on. The fact is that there is an enormous and diverse industry thriving on the backs of salmon and salmon fishermen.

Salmon fishing with rod and line on salmon beats provides direct employment and income for thousands of folk, and many more jobs in ancillary industries such as boat building, tackle and clothing manufacture, not to mention the retail outlets. The sport provided on salmon beats attracts foreign money and thousands of visitors to hotels in remote rural areas. It extends the opening season for these hotels beyond the normal tourist season. There is a spin-off to the local grocer, butcher, craft shop,

The River Orchy with Black Mount on the skyline. Sparkling water, clear skies and open moorland, but many upland flows have been severely affected by forestry plantings

petrol station and the rest because the modern sportsman tends to spend locally, unlike his counterpart of the past who might choose to lay on a special train to bring provisions from the great shops of London, who incidentally vied competitively for their trade. In these ancillary industries, the revenue gained from fishermen may be all that lies between profit and loss.

Several attempts have recently been made to estimate the income, for the Scottish economy alone, which can be directly attributed to salmon fishing. The great bulk of this comes from salmon beats in private ownership. Estimates range from £60 million to £140 million. If only one per cent of either of these sums was to be ploughed back into our rivers, how much could be done with the sum? How many netting companies could be bought out and their workforces employed on river management and enhancement? How many empty rivers could be returned to productivity, obstacles removed, spawning redds maximised and, as a result, extra income and further employment created? And what is the public's recognition of all this? Little more than a prohibitive bill for sporting rates. Oh yes, local authorities don't hesitate to leap on the sporting bandwagon! Just take the case of the Thurso as one example. As Lord Thurso reported in 1985, the Thurso pays £6,042 to Highland Region annually – a sum which takes one sixth of the angling rents and offers the angler little or nothing in return.

So this chapter, thus far, has done little but outline some of the problems faced on the salmon rivers and beats. Perhaps the times they are a'changing. It is to be hoped they are. Realising a full potential will need leadership and vision at the national as well as the local level.

In purely fish and fishing terms, one of the great causes for concern on many of the beats of classic salmon rivers has been the declining fortunes of early season fish, springers as they are called, the highly valued prizes of the opening months of the season. Over recent decades, apart from minor upswings in the mid and late seventies, the spring run, if not disappearing entirely, is little more than the faintest shadow of its former glory. This is seen at its worst on the Tay. Much the same is true on the great beats of the lower Spey, and even the Dee and Tweed are far from being able to approach their former reputations as producers of early season fish. How much of this is cyclical, it is hard to say. Certainly the pattern on Tweed is for a thirty-year cycle, swinging between spring and autumn runners, but the swing back to spring is already overdue. Other forces must be coming into play. The harvest on the high seas is still taking its toll. Drift netting off Ireland, legal drifting off Northumberland and illegal drifting off Scotland make further heavy inroads into already depleted spring stocks.

How much of this is tied up with the ever increasing runs of summer salmon and grilse into the classic rivers? This phenomenon will grow still further as more and more coastal and estuary nets are bought out – nets which have, in the past, taken incredible harvests of salmon during the low-water summer months. Some authorities have argued the theory of the 'over-cutting' of redds, stating their belief that summer and autumn runners, arriving on the spawning redds after the springers, simply destroy the eggs of the early fish. This has been used as an argument to increase netting activities during summer and autumn, to remove the supposed competition to spring fish. I do not hold with this theory and fear that man, in an attempt to manipulate salmon runs by increasing the commercial harvest, is not only using a questionable, at best, management tool, but one which could easily back-fire in his face.

It would be foolish to be dogmatic about future prospects for salmon stocks and fishing on the classic rivers and great beats. There are far too many imponderables and uncertainties for any man with the faintest touch of sanity to stick his neck out too far. And yet, as I said in an earlier book, history and my own experience of salmon have shown them to be survivors, even in the face of the most damning odds. It will be up to all those involved in salmon fishing with rod and line to do what they can to ensure that streams, rivers, estuaries, coasts and high seas are nurtured and managed for the maximum benefit and productivity of salmon, and sport for ourselves. The will and depth of feeling is perhaps greater now than ever before. It gives confidence that there is a great future for salmon fishing and the preservation of the reputations and some of the finer traditions of the great salmon beats.

Salmon leaping a weir on the Hampshire Avon – there can be a great future for the fishing if the will and depth of feeling is great enough

The Bisterne Water on the Hampshire Avon. Salmon fishing is of social importance in the south of England, but rural communities are not economically dependent upon it

CHAPTER 2

SALMON BEATS – SOCIAL AND ECONOMIC

Salmon beats, and fishing in general, play a substantial role in the social history and economies of many of the more remote, rural areas. It is hard to say just how much, in purely financial terms, they contribute to the nation's wealth. However, as we have seen, for Scotland alone figures ranging between £60 million and £140 million have been suggested. They provide work where other employment may be hard to find. They are part of our traditional rural life. And, of particular interest in this day and age, they provide recreation for hundreds of thousands of people.

In looking at the historical, legal and social background to salmon beats, as so many of them are to be found in Scotland, it seems sensible to concentrate on the country where their value has been clearly recognised since 1318 when they first became the subject of legislation. The right to fish for salmon in Scotland, whether in a river, estuary or on the coast, belonged originally to the Crown. From an early stage these rights, particularly for fishing in rivers, were conveyed to individuals by means of written Crown grants. And it is from these original grants that private title to salmon fishing must be derived.

Salmon fishing rights in Scotland are not dependent on the ownership of adjoining land. They are described as a separate heritable right and, as such, can be sold or leased separately. The exception to this rule occurs in Orkney and Shetland. There may be no great salmon beats in these islands off the north coast of Scotland. However, what migratory fish are caught in these parts are taken under the protection of udal tenure, dating back to the time when they were Norwegian territory. Under udal tenure, salmon fishing is attached to ownership of the land, and not a separate inheritable estate. For exactly the same reason, those fishing great salmon beats on the mighty rivers of Norway may find that the proprietor is a co-operative of small farmers. In this day and age, with some of the rents paid to fish the Norwegian rivers, one can be in little doubt as to whether farming or fishery ownership is their most valued asset.

For an understanding of the historical background to the beats, it is necessary to realise that the notion of catching salmon for sport, as any sort of a serious proposition, is a relatively new development. Indeed, the early grants of rights to fish for salmon were nothing more than a right to harvest a wild crop, by net, cruive or spear, for consumption by man and beast. Farming in the remoter parts of Scotland was never easy, but life was helped by this ready source of high protein food. Smoked salmon, now considered a delicacy, was nothing more than a suitable way of preserving that protein to see people through the harsh days of winter.

The modern gourmet-glutton might get quite excited at the thought of salmon as a staple diet, but not so the people of an earlier age. When apprentices finally tired of a never-ending diet of salmon flesh, laws were enacted limiting the number of times that it could be fed to them. It seemed a crime to waste the surplus. In some areas it was used to fatten pigs, and one can only wonder about the flavour of the milk in areas where it was used as winter fodder for cattle.

Crown grants were originally made to landowners who played a significant role in the local economy and society. Where a river was small, the entire fishing rights from source to estuary might be granted to one proprietor. In other cases, on larger rivers, the recipients of the grants might receive the right to fish only a certain stretch, normally that part of the river contained within the boundaries of their land. Here we see the birth of the salmon beats of today – sections of a river where one proprietor has the established right to fish and may lease that right to others.

It was not until the nineteenth century that salmon fishing with rod and line was taken seriously. This was at a time when the British Empire was reaching its zenith. Many of the early sportsmen who ventured north in pursuit of sport were colonial officers or military men home on leave from far-flung corners of the globe. With time hanging heavy on their hands after the first, brief novelty of London and home, they sought out fresh air and exercise with that zeal and fervour which, today, we cannot fail to associate with the Victorian era. Planning a sporting trip to the remoter Highlands at that time, where wild clansmen spoke a foreign tongue and were still not long settled after the last attempt to put the Stewart Kings back on the throne which ended in bloody defeat at Culloden Moor in 1746, probably seemed as great an adventure as an elephant hunt in the lands of the Karamajong. Not quite as risky, and certainly not as profitable, but an adventure all the same!

Landowners, lairds as they are called in Scotland, were not slow to see an opportunity to increase their incomes. Others, in need of greater boosts to their funds or simply from man's inherent inability to recognise the potential of what he holds, were quick to sell their estates to a new generation of sportsmen made wealthy through international trade.

Some of the original landowners, perhaps the great majority, decided to hold on to what they had, or at least to keep it in the family. A clear example of this is to be seen on the Thurso river, in Caithness. The situation there is described more fully in Chapter 7 but, to summarise, the original Crown grant was made to the Earls of Caithness. In their turn, they passed on these rights to a branch of the family, the Sinclairs of Ulbster, in the early eighteenth century. Nearly two hundred seasons of food harvests passed before Sir Tollemache Sinclair turned his thoughts to developing the river as a sporting, income-generating resource. Today, although the management of the river has been formed into a company to avoid the worst effects of taxation, the Thurso is still effectively controlled by Lord Thurso, direct descendant of Sir Tollemache and the original Sinclairs of Ulbster.

Besides those who took the money and ran, ownership of salmon fishings was to change for other reasons, in many cases. The social history of landed estates, since

River Findhorn at Dulsie Bridge. Popularised by Charles St John, the Victorian sportsman-writer, such rivers were a growing attraction as the railway opened the previously inaccessible Scottish Highlands to southern sportsmen

their heyday at the turn of the century, shows the general pattern of a downward spiral. Many lairds, in the face of uncertainty or unbearable financial pressure due to the burden of taxation, saw no alternative but to sell the whole or at least part of their estates. The traditional lairds of Highland estates were not inherently wealthy men, except in terms of the land they held and then only when it became valuable. Some of them learnt the modern commercial ways, but others went to the wall. A new breed emerged to buy up what the old lairds had lost, either voluntarily or otherwise. The wealthy, upper-middle class of merchant traders had become super-wealthy. Along with the beginnings of a new distribution of wealth, we see the start of a redistribution of salmon fishing and beats into new ownership.

This sets the stage for the rest of twentieth-century development. It opens with a range of traditional lairds from the wealthiest down to those just hanging on by the skin of their teeth, plus a good smattering of those labouring under the description of 'nouveau riches' but who could take a quiet satisfaction in knowing that, by and large, they were the wealthiest of all.

Since that time, and throughout the present century, most landowning families have faced one problem after another. Individual lairds have had their own sets of problems, but there is a common thread running through most of their histories. At its most basic, it is a tale of dwindling wealth, rather than merely dwindling income, in the face of ever increasing costs. And the reason why it is a tale primarily concerned with dwindling wealth is that no estate could be run in the old style and expect to make a profit. Income from wealth outside the estate was required in order to carry the loss. For these reasons, it is not impossible to caricature the progress of traditional landowners in the last century.

Many present-day lairds have inherited a property that has been in their family for more than a century. Subsequently, they have discovered that the expectation of managing the estate in the style of their wealthier ancestors is a financial burden too heavy to bear. Their personal financial position may have improved significantly throughout the 1980s, but they wonder how long this trend can continue and are deeply concerned for the future of sport, farming and forestry.

Most lairds, other than those with extensive estates or those barely scratching a living, feel themselves fortunate to have business interests outside the estate, or to have developed the estate's potential beyond its normal sphere of forestry, farming and sporting activities. Many will freely admit that without the income they derive from these outside interests, they would seriously have to consider selling at least part of the estate. In their gloomier moments, perhaps some will think they might be a great deal better off and carry less responsibility without their estate.

So why don't they sell? The fact is that many lairds, having inherited an estate, will feel that, whatever the legality of the situation, they have no moral right to dispose of the property. They see themselves as little more than guardians of a legacy to be passed on to future generations.

Yes, some will say, but surely this is utter nonsense. They see the laird, an apparently wealthy man with his house and its contents, his gardens and thousands

River Carron below the falls near Braelangwell Lodge. Shrouded behind this traditional scene on salmon rivers is a socially and economically significant rural history

of acres of ground, his shooting, fishing and stalking, and say: 'There sits a wealthy man'. The facts are not quite so simple. Apart from the pride and pleasure of ownership, his wealth is tied up. The value of his fixed assets may be more than considerable but unless he is prepared to sell some of those assets, what matters that to him? The fact that his salmon beat or whatever is worth ten thousand or ten million is of only passing interest to a man who sees himself as the guardian for future generations. In fact, in terms of Capital Transfer Tax, its increasing value is little more than a headache.

But what about the income he can gain from these assets? If it were simply a matter of slipping the income directly into his bank account then yes, he would be a very wealthy man. However, he will soon be having to write cheques to cover the annual running costs of the asset. Where such an asset is not realising its maximum potential, or is incapable of doing so, expenses may exceed income. Now, a loss could be happily borne in the days when landowners, on the whole, had at least some reserves of capital outside the estate, whether as the result of foreign trade or whatever; but in many families a couple of generations of taxation have eaten up whatever outside surplus wealth was available. Particularly since World War II, these surplus funds have dwindled to nothing in a number of cases and, on the death of one generation, the successor has been forced to sell off at least a part in order to keep what he can. For this reason, more than a few salmon beats have changed hands. They are the obvious asset to dispose of to ensure that the overall pattern and holding of the estate is not upset too drastically.

How is it possible to make a loss on, say, a salmon beat? The answer is that, particularly where a full-time gillie is employed, it is a fairly simple matter. With the gillie's cottage, which might otherwise have been sold or let, his wages and national insurance, and perhaps some transport, a telephone and whatever, he will be costing the estate a considerable sum each year. Then there are sporting rates, which might cost another couple of thousand. And some annual maintenance costs are practically unavoidable. Let us suggest a total figure in the region of £10,000. What does this sum represent for, say, a Highland river beat which enjoys a trickle of sport in the opening months of the season, building to a crescendo with summer salmon and grilse – a lettable season of some five months? Of course, the rent for the summer weeks will be highest but, on average, the beat must produce an income of £2,000 per month, say £500 per week, and that is simply to break even.

A proportion of the spring weeks, when the chances of catching a salmon are slim, will remain unlet. Those that are let may be to a couple of guests paying something in the region of £75, so it doesn't take much of a mathematician to deduce that the summer weeks will have to produce in the region of £1,000 per week, and again this is just to break even. The laird and his estate will lose nothing but, there again,

River Inver in Sutherland. On such West Highland rivers, which can show excellent sport but only over a limited period, fishing economics can be marginal if a full-time gillie with no other duties is employed

neither do they profit. Without profit, lacking any sort of reward for his capital investment, time and effort, unless the laird is a man of considerable private means and benevolent attitude, it is difficult to predict the economic survival of the beat and the future of the gillie who is employed.

There is, however, another side to this gloomy picture. Salmon and the beats where they are caught can just as easily be recognised as part of a multi-million leisure industry. So far, what has been discussed are those beats that might be able to produce an income approaching £1,000 a week at their peak times. There are some great beats which, in fact, can produce this rental income in a single day. Some produce it in a morning. The rent of £15,000 per week for 5 rods on, say, a Tweed beat in autumn shows the sums that can be paid.

At this stage of the argument some people will not be happy with the discussion. After all, most of us would prefer not to have our sport sullied by lengthy financial discussions. Better to pay the rent, then forget about it and go and enjoy oneself.

That attitude is all very well, but if this book were to ignore the economic realities, it would not provide a general picture of salmon beats with any degree of accuracy. So many people recognise the 'what' without understanding the 'why' and it is so easy for the facts to become mixed up with the myth and legend of salmon fishing. Many people still talk about 'sport fishing' and 'commercial fishing' when what they really mean is fishing with rod and line as opposed to fishing with net and coble. In reality, both involve commercial activities. One of the problems in convincing government and other bodies of the need to protect rod and line interests is that they see fishing with a rod as a fun activity whereas, with a net, men's livelihoods and business investment are at stake. This is utter nonsense. Of the two activities, the rod and line industry is far and away the more important, employing far more people, involving a far larger capital investment, creating greater income, funding local authorities and attracting tourism. Taking salmon in a net is an out-dated anachronism and, unless it can be seriously justified for other than commercial reasons, it ought to be stopped tomorrow and its work-force, numbering less than one thousand, absorbed into hatchery work, river improvement or whatever on the heels of an increasingly buoyant rod and line industry.

The figures are well known. A salmon taken in a net has only 1–2 per cent of the value to the economy of the same fish taken by rod and line. In other words, £2,000 worth of salmon, to the estuary netsman, may represent £100–200,000 to the upstream rod and line industry.

Sit in a fire-side chair with a dram of whisky and dream the dream of Old Scotia. Mists swirl over craggy mountains where a warrior race stride out in tartan kilts, fortified by porridge, haggis and kippers for breakfast and whisky with everything. Such is the stuff of the legend as portrayed on biscuit tin lids and tourist board posters. Hold the dream of Victorian sportsmen fishing, shooting and stalking their way across the Highlands, from coast to coast, for little more than letters of introduction. But for goodness' sake, and the sake of the future of rivers, beats and salmon, be aware of at least some of the modern economic realities of the sport.

CHAPTER 3

GILLIES AND THEIR GENTLEMEN

Virtually all the great salmon beats have one or more gillies, or 'ghillies' as it is sometimes spelt. Originally the word meant the most trusted companions and personal retainers of a Highland chief, there to protect his sides and back in times of peace and war. All this talk in dictionaries about their being 'servants' of the chief is misleading but understandable when you come to realise that Highland society was based on a fraternal and paternal system – a totally different concept from the feudal system introduced to England by the Normans. However that may be, the term gillie is used today to describe the professional companions of gentlemen – and ladies, of course – fishing a beat.

What is their purpose? At its most basic, it can be said that they are there to advise the guests and help them to catch fish. Salmon are not caught here, there and everywhere on a beat, and it can take many seasons, possibly a life-time of annual visits, to discover where the best salmon lies are, how best to fish them, when and with what. As J. Hughes-Parry wrote in his book *Fishing Fantasy*:

> Even on the river that one knows well, each pool has to be treated separately, and all one can do is keep an open mind and learn what is possible from the specialists, always remembering that the more one is willing to learn the better chance one has of becoming one of the few who can hold their own on any and all rivers.

How do you recognise a good gillie? Most of the best ones seem to have been raised on the river, or at least in the area; but this is not always true. Again, most of them are expert salmon fishermen in their own right; but this does not mean they will make a good gillie any more than the qualification of place of birth. Neither can you stereotype the perfect gillie by his appearance, any more than you can judge a sausage by its skin, although you should be wary of those who look as if they have just stepped out of the window of some fashionable high street store, slipping out of their Gucci slippers and into their designer polaroids before donning knee-length wellingtons. Good gillies can be scruffy or smart, young or old; they may be cheerful and jokey or serious and quiet. It is not how they look, it is what they know that counts.

One of the best definitions of the perfect gillie is set out in R. N. Lochhead's *With Rod Well Bent*:

> He will know the river to the very last stone and eddy, and knowing it, he will be ready and able to guide your wading steps and searching fly. He will not, however, be a school-

A spring salmon in the gillie's net

Five perfectly fresh-run salmon – the fine reward of fishing one great salmon beat

master, seeking to bend your style and inclination to his will, but ready to appreciate your whims and fancies, for salmon fishing is your pleasure and not your livelihood.

That, certainly, is all that the experienced fisherman requires of his gillie; to be told where the salmon are to be found on the beat, and to be advised of any pitfalls in wading it. Beyond that, except to the more elderly fisherman, whether or not the gillie leaps forward to carry rod and fishing bag pales into insignificance. Neither, for the experienced fisherman, should it matter too much whether the gillie is on hand to land hooked fish, and so there is little problem in sharing a gillie with others fishing the beat. Personally, I do not like a gillie to be constantly talking over my shoulder and, while I would never be so stupid as to ignore his advice, neither do I feel the need for a running commentary on what I should be fishing, nor how I should be fishing it.

Not all gillies are paragons of virtue. Far from it. As with all men, some gillies are simply born bad, while others are made that way. It is some of the 'gentlemen' who can cause real problems. They are ambitious not to catch one fish or two, but to go on to catch ten, and then twenty. And they expect their gillie to do all in his power to catch these fish for them, his brains with their hands on the rod. Older gillies of the best type may simply shake their heads at such antics; others do not. As Richard Waddington wrote in *Salmon Fishing: Philosophy and Practice*:

> There is little doubt that many good gillies are spoilt by visiting anglers. Many fishermen give their gillies far too much whisky and too much freedom of expression. I know one or two gillies who are so accustomed to being treated as 'Delphic Oracles' that it is practically impossible for any self-respecting man to have anything to do with them.

Also, as Hugh Falkus so rightly observed in his *Salmon Fishing*:

> Gillies on some of the big beats today are invested by absentee fishery owners with an authority that not all are able to exercise without insolence. It is, I suppose, symptomatic of the times.

This is undoubtedly true, and it can be seen in some gillies' attitudes as well as their spoken word. Let me offer the case of my wife's cousin and her husband. They were staying on Speyside for a week of mixed grouse shooting and salmon fishing. Karen had never fished in her life, but Charles quickly showed her how to use a spinning rod and fixed-spool reel. In the meantime, the gillies moved off with the more experienced fishers in the party, who really didn't need them – certainly not as much as a raw novice on her first day's fishing.

After a while, Karen, realising that she was delaying Charles from fishing and now being able to cast a Devon minnow at least in the right direction, sent him off to

(Top) *The younger generation – older fishermen hold the salmon resource in trust for them*

(Bottom) *The larger class of carbon rod reigns supreme for fishing the great salmon beats*

Gentleman and gillie fishing a rocky pool on the Cassley. Gillies should be regarded as fishing companions and guides

A fine salmon from the Oykel – fruit of a very special relationship

leave her to practise. Charles moved on to the next pool. You will probably have guessed the outcome. Twenty minutes later, a breathless lorry driver came stumbling down the river bank and called to Charles to 'come and help the lady land her salmon'. Great rejoicing. Karen had hooked and played a salmon entirely on her own, and all Charles had to do was to scoop the salmon out of the river for her.

Then Charles was told by one of the gillies that the arrangement was that, in addition to the set tip of £5 per day, there was an additional payment to the gillie of £5 per fish (this was a few years ago). Charles was furious, the gillies not having even seen the fish until it was on display in the hall of the lodge, let alone having played any part in its capture. However, he was told by the rest of the party that this was the way things were done, and given the distinct impression that to do otherwise could result in some sort of a gillies' strike. And so he paid the extra £5. As he said, the tip came to what he had planned to give anyway; it was just that he didn't think much of being told that he must pay it. Anyway, the beat and the party had to find another couple for the following year.

But that's enough about bad gillies. While it cannot be denied that they exist, they are, fortunately, the exception and, make no mistake, a great deal rarer than unbearably rude and conceited gentlemen! The truth of the matter, for most regular visitors to great salmon beats is, as Richard Waddington has also said:

> Many gillies are, by comparison, perfectly delightful, and I am glad to say that some of the pleasantest memories of my own fishing are associated with the personalities and conversation of some of the gillies with whom I have been privileged to fish.

In more recent times, Neil Graesser in *Advanced Salmon Fishing* describes his encounter with one gillie who did not come up to the mark in what R. N. Lochhead described as 'ready to appreciate your whims and fancies', but he added:

> In a long career on the banks of many rivers I have only on the oddest of occasions met with anything except politeness and courtesy from a ghillie, and this particular ghillie, I can only assume, wanted to impress me with his knowledge of the beat.

So there we are.

The gillie's prime function is, as has already been said, to ensure that his gentlemen and ladies have the best possible chance of catching a fish. In addition, it helps if he is something of an extrovert and an optimistic character. When the new guest arrives and enquires how the fishing is going, he doesn't really want to hear that he might as well have stayed at home and cast his flies into a bucket; even if it is the truth. For the fisherman, there is nothing worse than hearing such news.

On the other hand, there are few things more irritating, after a couple of days of it, than hearing

> Sure sir, you're bound to be catching a fish in this next pool, you being such a grand fisherman with all that wonderful tackle. That's the way of it now, sir; just next to that

rock and you'll have him . . . Sure they're being the sulky boys today, but I don't doubt
you will be catching one on those marvellous flies of yours; quite murder on the fish.

This has been heard from more than one Irish gillie when the river was bank high,
the fish had all run upstream, and you might as well have tried to pick daffodils in
December as catch a fish. Somewhere, there is a happy medium; a note of cautious
but realistic optimism. It may be no more than: 'There's aye a daft yin about', even
if that leaves you wondering whether the gillie is speaking about the salmon or
yourself.

At times, maintaining some sort of optimism must be an unenviable and frustrating
task for the gillie. There are times on the beats when salmon will be caught, almost
in spite of any antics that the fishermen may get up to. There are other times, even
on the greatest of salmon beats, when conditions have been driven beyond hope.
Equally, as demand for salmon fishing, whether it be good, bad or indifferent,
continues to rise, more and more folk are fishing beats at the wrong time of the
season. They may offer marvellous sport for a few months, but be virtually useless
outside these times.

A couple of seasons ago, I was having a dram with a gillie on a Highland river.
The time was early October, long after the river had been able to produce fresh run
fish. He had guests fishing, but could raise no enthusiasm for taking stale, coloured
fish, fish which we both agreed should be left unmolested. He was just going through
the motions of accompanying them and, as he said, 'It upsets me. You would think
that folk like that would know better.'

What are the things that a gillie looks for on his beat to produce good fishing?
Firstly, and most obviously, it will be the arrival of fresh, clean fish. He will look to
the water temperature but not be over-concerned so long as it is not at the extremes
– neither too hot nor too cold, preferably between about 40 and 55°F for best results.
Even more important is the water height, and the gillie will not want to see his
fishermen dawdling on the river bank during the first inches of a rise nor when a
spate has cleared and is falling.

When such conditions occur, what does he expect of his gentlemen? Firstly, it is
sheer mechanical efficiency; the ability to cast a good, long line and fish it well.
Gillies, however, are far from expecting all their guests to be tournament casters or
even particularly polished performers and, in normal circumstances, many of them
will not mind spending a little time (if they are asked pleasantly to do so because it
is well outside the scope of their normal duties), in giving some advice on casting.
However, it is only understandable that when the beat is hotching with fish and
conditions are perfect for catching them, they can quickly grow impatient with a
completely inept caster.

Moreover, someone who has not learnt to cast properly may not only be a nuisance
but a positive danger as well. For example, fishing the deep, slow dubs of Tweed
puts a premium on casting technique when fast-sinking lines and big heavy flies are
the standard outfit, at the opening and close of the season. On those occasions when

Gillies also act as boatmen. Here, on the lower Spey near Fochabers, the boat is being let down the current on a rope

Gillies are not only a Scottish phenomenon: fishing the Vanstone Pool of the Goodrich Water of the Wye

a gillie shares a boat with his fisherman, if that fisherman cannot cast, the gillie is likely to end up with a Yellow Dog or Willie Gunn earring. In particularly bad cases, gillies have sensibly refused to continue until the fisherman has practised well out of harm's way. Two inches of brass tube, armed with a large treble hook and moving at the speed of a bullet, is not something to be taken lightly.

There is one other thing that a gillie might hope for from the guests who come to his beat. It doesn't seem too much to ask – nothing more than a little human consideration and respect. Yet, at times, it is sadly lacking. There are times when I have been left literally cringing at the way a few guests think they can talk to and treat a gillie. One small example might be the way many guests imagine that the correct way to address a gillie is by his surname alone. Life is hard, but is made much more bearable by 'Would you mind giving me a hand with this, Alec', instead of 'Take this, MacDonald'. Why is it that, for some people, a visit to the country and contact with country people is like entering some sort of a time warp? 'In days of old, when knights were bold and peasants were downtrodden.'

Sometimes, of course, the whole thing can be put down to cultural differences. For example, on North American rivers the general attitude is that drink and fishing don't really mix. If the guests are going to take a drink with their gillie, or guide as they might prefer to call him, it will be at the end of the day. Some Scottish gillies, on the other hand, prefer a drip feed to a flood. Whatever the reason, and if ever this can be an excuse, it has given rise to what has probably become the most famous of gillies' tales.

A bitterly cold day on the Spey, Tay, Tweed or wherever, depending on which man is telling the tale. The gillie has an American guest and, seeing that he is armed only with a short, single-handed rod, it is obvious that they will have to fish continuously from the boat in order to cover the river adequately. No matter, the gillie is well used to spending long hours at the oars, holding the boat in the stream.

As the day wears on, and the weather becomes even more wretched, the gillie is not so much aware of the American's fishing ability as of the fact that, at regular intervals, he is taking a hefty drink from a big shiny flask, filled with the nectar of the glens. He is also managing to demolish a large number of the finest cigars. However, when he goes to light yet another in the late afternoon, he finds that his box of matches is completely sodden. Throwing the useless matches into the river, he turns on the gillie.

'Jock, is there nowhere dry in this goddamned country of yours?', he demands.

The gillie fixes him a steely stare. 'Weel now, sir, you could be trying the back of my throat', is the 'porky' reply.

Such gillies' tales are endless, and long evenings, when gillies gather together for a dram and to swop their stories, are broken with great roars of laughter. Only one small group is spared from the gillies' tales, and that is the Royal Family. No gillie will discuss their doings, not if he is worthy of his craft. Politicians and industrialists, the military and the professions yes, but never the Royal Family. On that there is a code of silence that would put the Mafia to shame.

CHAPTER 4

FROM LANCEWOOD TO CARBON-FIBRE

The development of fishing tackle through the centuries has had a fundamental effect on salmon fishing. In the same way that the development of driven game shooting followed on the heels of the invention of the breech-loading ejector shotgun, so sport on the great salmon beats has been fashioned closely on the rods, reels and lines available in their time.

The fishing rod originated in Egypt. It has been used there for thousands of years. However, it was not until fairly recent times that it developed beyond a 'stick and a piece of string'. Try to imagine what would happen if a large and lively salmon were hooked on such gear. No wonder that Gervase Markham, when he wrote *The Pleasure of Princes* in 1614, described the salmon as:

> Unfit for your travaile, both because he is too huge and cumbersome, as also that he naturally delighteth to lie in the bottoms of the great depe Rivers, and as neare as may bee in the midst of the Channel.

Clearly, with the relatively crude tackle of the Middle Ages the fisherman was not only unable to present his lure to salmon any distance out from the bank, but it was also unlikely that he could hope to come out on top in the ensuing struggle.

However, within forty years of Gervase Markham saying that the salmon was not suitable for the fisherman's efforts, we find a reference to the fishing reel, then presumably a recent introduction to Europe from China. Thomas Barker in *The Art of Angling* which appeared in 1651 describes a long hazel rod with a 'Ring of Wyre' at its top for the line to run through and a 'winde to turne with a barrell, to gather up his Line and loose at his pleasure'.

After the introduction of these early reels, even if ratchet pawls were still undreamt of, the defeat of a fish as 'huge and cumbersome' as a salmon had become a distinct possibility. Even so, the early salmon reel bore no more than a passing resemblance to its modern counterpart. Made of brass in a size fit for the king of fish, it would weigh in the region of 2lb.

Rods, of necessity, had to be long. Lines in those days were made of plaited horse-hair. They simply lacked the weight for effective casting, and fishermen had to rely heavily on 'dibbling' the fly beneath the tip of their rods. Obviously, the longer the rod, the further out the fly could be dibbled and, hence, the popularity of rods of 18, 20 or more foot in length.

Popular timbers for these rods were lancewood, hickory, beech and poplar. Such

A fine September salmon from Tweed. Gervase Markham, writing in 1614, warned that the salmon was 'too huge and cumbersome' to take on the rods and lines of his era

a weapon was as thick as a man's arm at its butt. Ally such a pole to the heavy reel of the time and the result was something that could only have been wielded for the very shortest of times, except by the exceptionally fit and strong. Little wonder that the majority view of the time was that cruive, net or spear were the only sensible means of extracting a harvest of salmon from the river. It was this fundamental lack of adequate tackle, as much as anything, that retarded the development of salmon fishing with rod and line as a sport.

Things changed little up to the middle of the nineteenth century, when Thomas Tod Stoddart was obviously still keen on lancewood for rod building:

For top-pieces it is reckoned invaluable, possessing a spring and consistency, together with a capability of being highly polished, not found in any other wood.

However, towards the end of the century, most fishermen had rejected all timbers other than greenheart and cane for their rods. This factor, together with the introduction and adoption of silk lines with the intrinsic weight for satisfactory casting, can be seen as the real turning point toward fly fishing techniques as we know them today. After the turn of the century, however, one fascinating factor emerged. Up to that time, gentlemen and gillies had fished with almost identical tackle and in the self-same style. Then, with some exceptions of course, the gillies chose the greenheart and stuck with long rods, whilst the gentlemen, spurred on by Arthur Wood of Cairnton who was regarded as some sort of a fishing messiah in the earlier part of this century, plumped for shorter, stiffer cane rods. What makes it all the more intriguing is that, after a parting of the ways for nearly three quarters of a century, when gillies' and gentlemen's tackle and techniques have once again, in modern times, become indistinguishable, it is the gillies, rather than the gentlemen, whose decision has stood the test of time. Today, nobody thinks twice about fishing with a 15ft rod on the famous salmon rivers and beats. Twenty years and less ago, gentlemanly writers spoke of the 'ridiculously long, weaver's beams of yesteryear'. Many will today fish happily with a carbon-fibre rod of 17ft or more.

All this, and the various reasons for it, are described in the later chapters on fly fishing methods. So are the outstanding but often unsung successes of men like Alexander Grant, 'Wizard of the Ness' and inventor of the Grant Vibration rod. He may not have been a gillie, but he was a born and raised Highlander. His views on tackle, therefore, can be taken as fairly representative of one side of what became a north-south division of opinion in the late nineteenth and early twentieth centuries. What *were* his views on tackle?

Grant used a long rod, as long a rod as he could comfortably handle. He was singularly unimpressed by the tackle advocated by Arthur Wood. Most professional gillies agreed with him, it appears. 'Aweel, thae rods are richt eneuch for you gentlemen who come up here, but they won't stand us chaps', are the words attributed to them by Jock Scott in his book *Fine and Far Off*.

Whatever their exact words might have been, it is clear that many Highlanders considered the short cane rod and fishing in Wood's style as little more than the affectations of effete English trout fishermen, and the southern dry-fly fisherman in particular. Gillies saw their own role in life as being the catching and killing of salmon, and they chose what they believed to be the most efficient tool for the job. To most of them, this meant a rod at least 16ft. The longer rod of 17–18ft was very popular and some, Alexander Grant included, regularly cast and fished with rods of 20ft.

Such a length of rod, if made of greenheart, would weigh in excess of 30oz but the northern fisherman was prepared to tolerate this in order to obtain the incredible casting range and water command offered by such a weapon. It was with a rod of 21ft that Grant made his longest recorded cast – the colossal distance of 65yd. No line was shot; the entire length was picked up off the water and thrown.

This event took place on the River Ness in 1895 at a casting competition organised

by Mr Corballis, a magistrate residing at Moniack Castle. Besides his legal duties,
    Equally, and as already mentioned, it was the raw material as well as the sheer
length of rod which set the Highlanders apart from their southern gentlemen.
Returning to Jock Scott in his *Fine and Far Off*:

> Personally, I am all for the greenheart salmon rod. It is not fashionable, but I still believe
> it to be unbeatable at its job. The southron loves his split bamboo (dry fly influence
> again, I suggest) but I wish that he would take a tour round some of the really difficult
> rivers of Scotland – and some in England, too – the broad, fast and heavy rivers where
> salmon fishing is a man's job, look at the best fishers and notice what they use.

After those words, nobody can be in any doubt as to Jock Scott's feelings on the
subject. What did he have to say about the gillies of the great salmon beats?

> What about Highland ghillies? Spliced greenheart. And these men definitely prefer
> greenheart; it stands up to the work. Many a ghillie in the far north has been offered
> the gift of a split bamboo, and has declined it, so cost does not enter into the matter.
> The Ness and Spey experts use greenheart exclusively; and by experts I mean some of
> the finest fishermen I have ever seen, and I have seen a few.

Another writer to extol the virtues of the spliced greenheart rod was R. N.
Lochhead. One can only presume that his destiny was settled with his initials on his
christening day, for most of his book *With Rod Well Bent* concerns fishing adventures
during odd snatches of leave from the Royal Navy during World Wars I and II.
However, besides his tales of fish fought, won or lost, he spares a few lines to describe
his allegiance to the spliced greenheart rod:

> I have a goodly collection of salmon rods and they are all home made with one exception.
> The exception is a Grant Vibration spliced greenheart, and all my rods are copies of
> that well-known make. Once you have used one of these masterpieces of the rodmaker's
> art . . . then, I dare swear, you will be ready to discard all others and let the spliced
> greenheart be your constant companion and treasured friend.

So, with all this evidence stacked up in favour of the greenheart rod, why was it
that the split cane became the more fashionable choice, certainly for gentlemen
fishing the great salmon beats? Was it purely an affectation, or was there a great deal
of sense in their decision?
Corballis was a keen sportsman and the author of *Forty-five Years' Sport*, among
other books. He simply wanted to know what the Inverness experts could produce.
Competitors stood in an anchored boat, and cast straight downstream alongside a
measuring board to where Corballis and his companions stood by to mark the fall
of the fly. Incidentally, another man, Grant's closest rival and also using a 21ft rod,
cast the measured distance of 56yd. Both men used the switch cast, practically
identical to a single-Spey cast in the modern style, where fly, leader and only the very
shortest length of line just 'kiss' the water before the final throw.

A small Ayrshire river where sheer range in casting may be relatively unimportant

Richard Waddington – inventor of the famous style of fly which bears his name and helped so much in improving our success with salmon, particularly when fishing long flies in cold water – had access to some excellent water. He is also an accomplished writer on the subject of salmon and fishing. Probably the best known of his books is *Salmon Fishing: Philosophy and Practice* (1959) in which he clearly stated his views on the subject of greenheart versus split cane:

With a good greenheart Spey casting is far easier than with any split cane rod, and from my point of view, this advantage far outweighs any disadvantage that can be named . . .
Unfortunately, of every dozen that are made, on average, fully half are virtually useless. Another three or four are only fair, one is good, and one is very good. It is this variability in the quality of greenheart rods that, I am sure, has put many anglers off them.

There, in a nutshell, we discover the very real disadvantage of the greenheart rod. It was unpredictable. Now, it might be one thing for a gillie to make up, say, half a dozen rods at his workbench, trying them out, then taking them back to plane off a little bit here and there till at least one of them was entirely to his liking. Others, with less time and inclination, found it far easier simply to go to a top-class rod builder, where the quality of the split rods could be guaranteed and each one would be identical. The plain fact was that, while the best greenheart might indeed be a better rod than the best cane, a good cane rod was always better than the average greenheart.

Another point in favour of the cane rod was that, for the same length and power, it was considerably lighter than greenheart. For those fishermen who were happy to overhead cast most of the time, the cane rod avoided unnecessary weight and fatigue.

This is not to say that the cane rod cannot Spey cast. Many fishermen found that a rod like the spliced canes from Sharpes of Aberdeen did, in fact, perform very well in this respect. However, Spey and switch casts exert a tortional twist to the rod. The split bamboo cane rod is made up of six triangular strips, formed into a 'thrupenny-bit' shape and secured with glue. By continued twisting, caused by Spey casting over an extended period, the glue could become fatigued and the rod, quite literally, be torn apart. Greenheart, being solid, was not subject to this stress.

So things continued with little change in tackle for more than half a century on the great salmon beats. In general terms, the gillies stuck with their lovingly made long greenhearts, many of them Spey casting as standard practice, while their gentlemen bought best quality cane rods from firms such as Hardy Brothers or Sharpes. The gentlemen saw the Spey casts as a minor tactic, only to be used where absolutely necessary, when there was insufficient room to make a back-cast because of a high bank or riverside trees.

Next came fibre-glass. This had two main advantages over cane. It was lighter, and it was cheaper. Another advantage, but one that was possibly not all that widely recognised at the time was that, being tubular rather than glued, a fibre-glass rod could stand up better to the rigours of Spey casting. Gillies, as well as gentlemen, took quickly to the new fibre-glass.

In hindsight, it is a little surprising that with the introduction of fibre-glass, there was no immediate increase in rod length. The probable reason was that the fishing public had become so used to the well-worn formula of a 12ft rod for the floating line and a 14ft rod for the sinker, that there was little demand for the tackle trade to offer them anything else. Not so the gillies. A number of them, unable to obtain a length of rod to replace their greenhearts, took to buying fibre-glass blanks and rather than putting the corks for the handle straight onto the blank, made up a separate handle with a spigot fitting for the blank butt. Thus they easily converted a 14ft rod to 16ft and so on.

By now it was the late sixties and, while one section of society felt that there was nothing to beat long hair, beads and widely flared velvet trousers, another thought there was nothing to beat glass-fibre. The first group, a little older now, might still

Gaffing a spinner-caught salmon on the Wye at Caemawr. On most rivers in recent times, both gaff and spinner have lost in popularity

argue that they were right, but the other, the fishermen, were in for a surprise. Bruce & Walker, who had been the first to market and manufacture British-made fibre-glass rods had, by the mid-sixties, developed the first British prototype carbon-fibre rod.

The story of the introduction of carbon-fibre is not one of overnight success. The early years were full of tales and rumours of carbon rods cracking up without warning. Equally, because carbon-fibre is the same material as is used for lightning conductors, there were great fears for its safety if used close to overhead wires or carried during thunderstorms. In fact, there were some fatalities and close shaves, before people learnt the basic rules involved in safe handling. Above all, perhaps, the world of salmon fishing, and particularly that of the great salmon beats, can show a certain degree of conservatism. Change seldom comes easily but, by the late seventies, Bruce & Walker and their carbon rods were firmly established as the leader in the market.

Playing a Dee fish on the Jetty Pool at Aboyne with a modern, carbon fly rod

Originally, as happened in the case of fibre-glass, the principal advantage of carbon-fibre was seen in terms of its even greater saving in weight. For rods of equal length, cane had proved lighter than greenheart, fibre-glass lighter than cane, and now carbon-fibre was lighter still. Nobody needed to look much beyond that simple fact on beats and rivers up to medium size, such as the Awe, Findhorn, upper Dee, Deveron, Esk and so on.

However, on the great beats of the larger classic rivers such as the Tweed, Tay, Spey and on to the Ness, they were still echoing the words of Gervase Markham when he wrote in 1614 that the salmon 'naturally delighteth to lie in the bottomes of the great depe Rivers, and as neare as may bee in the midst of the Channel'.

The late John Ashley Cooper, widely accepted as the greatest fisherman of recent times to fish the great salmon beats, to which he seemed to have almost unlimited access, summed up the situation in his book *A Line on Salmon* published in 1983:

> The longer the rod (provided it has an effective action and is used with a line of the right weight), the longer the cast that can comfortably be made; and on a big river or even a medium one the ability to throw a long line whenever wanted is invaluable.

He wrote of the desirability of a cast of 35yd, and rejected rods of 14ft as being inadequate. He felt that as a 17ft carbon rod weighs less than a 14ft cane, which we had all been happy enough to fish with, there were no grounds for rejecting a long carbon rod of 16, 17 or even 18ft for use on the widest flows.

His words may sound like an almost century-old echo; Alexander Grant calling 'I told you so' from his grave. One thing has changed, of course. In Grant's day they spoke of their 17ft greenheart rods as hardly needing to exceed 30oz. My own 17ft tubular carbon-fibre rod weighs exactly half that amount, a mere 15oz; incidentally, my 16ft rod weighs 12oz and the 15ft just 10oz.

There are still some, of course, who question this need for long casting and will even seek to ridicule the exponents of the longer rods. However, those of experience do not; and neither do competent fishermen and gillies allow the thoughts of 'armchair anglers' to deter them from the road to success with salmon.

Beside the light weight of carbon, allowing long but light rods to be built and used, it has one other quality which has permitted a great change in accepted technique on many salmon beats, again, particularly, on the larger rivers. It may lack something of the character of natural material but, other than that, it is certainly the equal of, if not better than, greenheart when it comes to Spey casting. This has created another great revivalist movement on the salmon beats and there are many modern salmon fishermen who use the Spey cast exclusively. This cast puts yards onto the overhead, besides avoiding obstructions behind and virtually eliminating wind knots. It is also a far safer cast. Again, John Ashley Cooper was able to sum up the feelings of many modern salmon fishermen when he said:

> Personally, I have now for a number of years pretty well forsaken the overhead cast, except in exceptional circumstances, as being by comparison both clumsy and inefficient.

With the wide adoption of longer carbon rods on many beats, the more caring of the gillies who can still remember the techniques of fishing the cumbersome greenhearts have been able to explain some of the tricks of the trade for minimising fatigue. Any long rod, whatever the material, is a considerable lever and if, as has been the fashion started in the days of short cane rods, the rod is held with the end of the handle against the fisherman's stomach, this will be found to be very uncomfortable. A better practice with the longest rods is to hold the rod at its point of balance, just in front of the cork grip, with the grip running back along the forearm, between the elbow and side, and out behind. Such little tricks, long forgotten except by the older generation of gillies, relieve the back muscles and make fishing a pleasure rather than a chore. Nowadays, our long rods are so much lighter that such tricks may not be so important but, certainly with a rod over 16ft, they are useful to know. Today, the most popular rod in use on salmon beats is undoubtedly a 15ft carbon. Possibly a little too long for the smaller rivers, and perhaps not quite long enough for the stronger, wider flows, it is, nevertheless, an excellent all-round compromise for the one-rod man or woman.

Besides developments in fishing techniques brought about by changes in rod material, the other most significant advances must surely be in fly lines. As noted earlier, silk lines were not invented until the middle of the nineteenth century, and not widely adopted until slightly later. Silk had been available before, of course, but only in plaited form, as an alternative to plaited horse-hair. With these very light lines, it was practically impossible to cast any great distance, particularly against an adverse breeze, and most fishermen on the salmon beats had to resort to dibbling their fly almost directly beneath the rod tip. It was the introduction of silk lines in their braided, waterproof, oil-dressed form that revolutionised salmon fishing with the fly. Before the use of braided silk it would have been a good man indeed who could cast over 15yd. Then, within a very short time, we had a character like Alexander Grant being able to cast 65yd. It was the new braided silk, even more than the greenheart rod, which made this possible. Incidentally, if you are the type to take little interest in what so-and-so cast on such-and-such a date in competition, in practical fishing terms it is reported that Grant frequently hooked fish in high water with a huge 4/0 double iron at ranges up to 50yd.

The introduction of plastic lines to Britain, which I remember well as my father bought me one of the first from a Speyside tackle shop for my seventh birthday, may not have seemed such a consequential event as the earlier introduction of silk. The plastic floater was certainly a great deal more convenient than the silk line which had to be greased in order to make it float, but it was not until the introduction of a large array of various rates of sinking lines that the most beneficial effects were felt. Prior to this, the only way to adjust the fly's fishing depth was to increase its weight, which usually meant fishing a larger fly or using a heavier silk sinker.

Today, by changing from, say, an AFTM 10 medium sinker to an AFTM 10 fast sinker, the fisherman can fish deeper but still with the original fly. Equally, he could fish a smaller fly deeper still with an ultra-fast sinker. The possibilities and permutations are endless, and have done much to improve fishing tactics with the sunk line and long fly in cold water conditions. An indication of the impact of long carbon rods for Spey casting with range and control, plus the new generation of sinking lines, is the ever growing number of fishermen who have forsaken their spinning rods. Besides the fact that they prefer to cast and fish the fly, they have found that a well presented pattern such as the now legendary Willie Gunn will actually catch more fish than any form of spinner or spoon.

There is just one more obvious item of tackle to deal with, and that is the reel. Reels used for fly fishing are a fascinating subject and, indeed, whole books have been written about them. Possibly it is a reaction to modern life, or simply a desire to have one item of tackle that is not a product of space-age technology, but many a fisherman on the great salmon beats has been prepared to spend a small fortune to obtain a pre-war fly reel. It is not just collectors who are buying them up, it is practical fishermen as well.

Up to the late sixties, you could hardly give away second-hand fishing tackle. It had little, if any, value and however much it may horrify the modern fisherman even to consider the possibility, it has to be accepted that many reels were probably consigned to the rubbish heap by unknowing or uncaring fishing widows.

Others simply disappeared, in the way that these things do. I shall always remember the look on my father's face when he found an old reel of his in my grandfather's garden shed. It was loaded with string and had, for years, been used to ensure that rows of fruit and vegetables were planted in straight, regimented lines. The reel is a pre-war Hardy Perfect and, even after those years of abuse, it runs as smooth as the slickest silk. On finding this, my father began to remember other tackle that he had presumed lost in various moves, plus the war years. Grandfather mentioned a wicker creel, somewhere in the attics, and this turned out to be stuffed with old reels, some of them brass. There were also fly boxes and the like, although, unfortunately, the flies had been reduced to tattered remnants or bare hooks by the attention of generations of moths. Goodness knows what happened to the rods, but we have a sneaking suspicion that they may have been used to prop up rows of peas, and finally consigned to the bonfire. Such is life; at least we got the reels.

The clicking ratchet may not be the most efficient braking system in the world, and no engineer would suggest that it should, for example, be fitted in a car. But there is something about the song of the reel, its screams and screeches as a salmon bolts across a mighty pool, that will be forever an essential part of the whole fishing experience on great salmon beats.

So far in this chapter, practically all that has been written relates directly to the salmon beats in Scotland, but much the same progression – from greenheart to cane to fibre-glass and finally to carbon-fibre – can be related to the vast majority of those fishing the great beats of England, Wales and Ireland. Equally, much the same can be said of most Scandinavian countries, and Norway in particular with its roaring maelstroms of rivers which require long, double-handed and powerful fly rods as much, if not more than, any of the British flows.

In fact, the only major fishing area for Atlantic salmon where tackle can be said to be in direct contrast to what has been described is in North America.

A number of attempts have been made to introduce American tackle and techniques to the eastern side of the Atlantic and since, on such matters as rod lengths, they are so opposed to our own standard practice, they are worth looking at in some detail. There certainly seems to be a growth in interest in 'American-style' fishing among the great salmon beats, particularly those situated on rivers where the estuary and coastal nets have been bought-off, which is very likely to lead to a bonanza of sport with small summer salmon and grilse. It has to be recognised that, whereas in Britain we can fish an eleven-month salmon season, in North America their fishing is practically confined to the summer months. Therefore, while it can be said that they know very little of the problems of fishing a river such as the Tay at the start of our season, or the Tweed at its close, when it comes to summer fishing, we really should raise our hats to them as experts in their concentrated sphere of activity.

A neat summary of the American attitude towards fly rods for salmon fishing is given by that noted American sportsman, Lee Wulff, in his book *The Atlantic Salmon*:

> Rods over twelve-and-a-half feet are becoming relics now, used for sentiment. In their time there was no other way to cast a fly as far as easily. Modern rod materials and modern line tapers have increased the casting distance of the shorter rods and made the very long rods no longer necessary.

Naturally, this begs the question as to how short these 'shorter rods' he is talking about actually are. The fact is that Lee Wulff has hooked, played and beaten large salmon on a tiny rod just 6ft in length. Most people, even on his side of the Atlantic, would consider that to be taking things to extremes. From what one reads and hears, a rod of 9–10ft is the popular choice.

Their attitude is summed up again by L. James Bashline, former managing editor of *Field and Stream* magazine, in his book *Atlantic Salmon Fishing*:

> For ninety-five percent of the Atlantic salmon fishing in the world, a nine-foot rod casting a 9 weight line will do quite nicely.

He then goes on to say that there may be a place for 'the ponderous, two-handed salmon killers of European persuasion' and admits that he has spent some time slinging fly lines on prodigious poles of fourteen foot or more but adds:

> It is almost impossible to lay a fly down with finesse. These rods will fight a big fish to the beach in short order, but casting them and simply holding them for a full day requires the strength of a decathlon champion.

In our turn, we Europeans could 'split hairs' about such statements. Why should

An Oykel salmon. Americans prefer the shorter, single-handed fly rod. Shame about that beastly gaff!

it be any easier to cast a 9 line with finesse on a single rather than a double-handed rod? I use a 13ft double-handed with a 7 line for much of my delicate summer work, and that settles like thistle-down. Equally, I mentioned those comments about the strength of a decathlon champion to a dear old lady of 5ft 3in and close to seventy seasons who found it most amusing; in fact, she positively roared with laughter. She has fished many of the greatest salmon beats since her schooldays, normally with a 15ft rod, and her only concession to the passage of time has been to replace her greenheart with carbon-fibre!

But where nobody can argue with Jim Bashline is when he says that 'Fishing is supposed to be fun', and for a growing number of European sportsmen, particularly those raised on a diet of catching big trout from stillwaters on single-handed rods, the same rods for summer salmon fishing are all part of the game. Horses for courses, and one man's meat is another man's *poisson,* as the French would say.

Frost on the Hampshire Avon – the salmon season opens in the depths of winter

CHAPTER 5

EARLY SPRING AND AUTUMN FISHING

Salmon may suck on a worm or chew on a prawn, but it is almost universally accepted, outside 'flat-earth' circles, that salmon stop eating on their return to fresh water. Should we try to tease their curiosity, anger or defence mechanisms? If we seek to elicit some sort of conditioned feeding response, is this best achieved with a caricature of their prey at sea, or a memory of their time in the river as fry and parr? The questions are numerous, and possible solutions seem endless. We draw heavily on the experiences of both contemporary and past fishermen. Therefore, perhaps, in order to understand fully the ways of fishermen on the great salmon beats, we must know at least a little of what has gone before. Let us start with the case of a guest visiting the Spey at the turn of the century.

The kind host was a man of great experience of the Spey and its fishing who took a middle beat for the entire season. Equally, he recognised that his young guest was very much a novice but one who, with youth and strength on his side, should be able to master the heavy Castle Connel rod that he was to be lent. Indeed this was the case and, after a couple of shoulder-straining and back-breaking days the guest, under the tutelage of a fine old gillie, had learnt the rudiments of the Spey cast. Incidentally, the host would not allow any guest to fish without a gillie in attendance. He considered that, besides helping materially in the finding, catching and landing of salmon, a gillie was important because accidents could so easily happen on a rapid and powerful river like the Spey, even to the most agile of waders and strongest of swimmers.

The old-time Speyside gillies had more to do than pointing out where the salmon rested and saving the gentleman from drowning if he got carried away in pursuit of them. For example, the gillie's first job, before ever the guests arrived on the beat each morning, would have been to check over their tackle. He would already be thinking about what size and pattern of fly to start off with. With so many things to be remembered, young gillies learnt by heart a rhyme to ensure that nothing would be forgotten. While the host and his guests were sitting down to breakfast, the gillies would be in the Rod and Gun Room of the lodge, or in the fishing hut. Some would be muttering their rhyme to themselves as they picked up:

> Rods, reels and hooks,
> Nets, bait and baskets,
> Gaff, baton, books,
> Coats, lunch and flaskets.

Some of these items are self-explanatory; others are less so. The reference to hooks and bait shows that gillies and gentlemen of the time were prepared to resort to other means than the fly. The baton is what we now refer to as a priest – the truncheon-like weapon used to administer the last rites to the landed salmon. Incidentally, in Scotland, the correct word is 'grassed' rather than landed, no matter whether it be onto grass, rock, shingle or whatever. The books were not like the item you are now holding in your hand, useful only to while away the closed season and times when the salmon are not obliging. Their books were far more important. The pages were of felt, into which a great array of the classic salmon flies of the time were hooked. And heaven help the gillie who forgot the flaskets – flasks filled with whisky for his guests from the host's personal supply.

Do gillies like their whisky? I have heard that there are some who don't. Would they forgive a guest who failed to share a dram with them? Perhaps, if St Peter were fishing. Tied up with the vast majority of gillies' liking for a sensation is the story as to why so few of them will ever wear one of those Sherlock Holmes-style deer stalkers with ear flaps to be tied under the chin, 'twa snooters wi' lug flaps'.

One day, on the Aberdeenshire Dee, an old gillie was wearing one of these affairs. A gust of wind untied the bow holding the earflaps in place. Rather than go to the bother of retying them, the old gillie left them hanging. Later in the day, he realised that his gentleman was taking a good, big dram from the flask he produced from an inside pocket. The old gillie stared long and hard. 'Well, Duncan, I have offered you a dram three times today already, and you never said a word.' Realisation dawned. The ear flaps had stopped him hearing. In his anger the gillie flung the hat into the pool and, in his sorrow at missing three drams, he promptly jumped in after it and drowned himself.

So the story goes, but I digress.

Our guest to the Spey, having made his way down to the river, would have found his gillie waiting and ready with rod up and line threaded. Gut casts, fragile until soaked in water, would be lifted from a backwater and attached to the fly line before the fly book was opened and a choice made.

Let us say that it was April with the river fairly high, and cold but clear. The flies of the day were tied on big single hooks, 'salmon irons' as they were then called. The gillie guides his guest's choice away from the Thunder and Lightning with which he had caught a fish two days ago, when the river still carried a hint of colour, past the Gordon and Jock Scott, lingering over the last, and on to a Yellow Torrish dressed on a 6/0 iron. The gillie explains that while the day is cold, the sun is bright and still low on the horizon. In the slanting shafts of sunlight, a bright silver-bodied fly, like the Torrish, might work well.

For a few moments, before he passed it to the gillie for tying to the cast, the guest held the bright fly in his hand and wondered at its beauty. His eyes ran over it, taking in the tag of round silver tinsel and yellow floss silk behind the black ostrich herl butt and topping and ibis tail. He scanned its body, divided into two equal parts of embossed silver tinsel, separated by a butting of ostrich herl and Indian crow. Its

High water during the opening months on the Aberdeenshire Dee

yellow hackle blended with the built wing containing the plumage of white-tipped turkey tail, bustard, peacock wing, guinea fowl, golden pheasant tail, swan dyed red and blue, brown mallard and an irridescent topping of golden pheasant over all. The cheeks were of jungle cock and the neat, torpedo head was finished with a faultless skin of black varnish.

Ten minutes later, with an outer covering of heavy twill waders and stout leather wading brogues, the guest was in action. He had already seen a fish or two moving and, in another ten minutes, had felt a long pull which came to nothing. He had been warned about that. On the single hooks of the time, contacts with salmon included a liberal helping of fish touched, pulled or lost in the tussle to get them ashore.

Having fished out the pool, the guest came ashore to the waiting gillie. He was told that he was not doing too badly, but that he should try even harder to cast as long and straight a line as possible, and not to throw it at any greater angle than 45 degrees to the stream. Salmon in cold water, he was told, are lazy beasts, and you must endeavour to fish the fly as slow and as deep as possible if the salmon are to seize it.

And so he fishes on down the next pool where, towards the tail, he sees a fine fish throw itself close to the opposite shore. He is casting his best length of line but still fails to cover the fish. Should he cast more squarely to reach it? He looks back at his gillie. With a wave of the hand toward the opposite shore, the gillie shouts over the roar of the river. 'Gan in anither fit!' he advises. The guest does as he is bid, but with his heart beating wildly. Dislodged by his shuffling feet, stones the size of footballs roll for yards in the full rush of the Spey stream. He promises himself that he will stay for but three casts. On the second cast, the salmon takes with a real bang, almost toppling the fisherman.

The situation is serious. The gillie is on his feet and vigorously signalling to his charge to come ashore. 'Forget about the fish, man. Put yer rod ower yer shooder and let the bugger run.' Twenty-five minutes later, the guest's first lesson in playing a big salmon on a wide open river has come to an end. Gillie and guest are returning to a state of normality as they stand admiring an 18lb bar of gleaming silver and ebony. The gillie glances at his pocket watch.

'Aye sir, a bonny fish and ye handled him well. Aye indeed, no' much mair than a minute to the pun', and ye cannae expect better than that . . . Och well, sir, I dinnae mind if I do . . .'

That was the way of fishing the big fly in cold water conditions at the turn of the century and, to be honest, it is how we fish today at the same time of year. However, what has changed is the tackle that we use. Modern flies, lines and rods have revolutionised cold water fishing. And it was not all fly fishing – twenty or thirty years ago, for the vast majority of British fishermen on salmon beats, cold water fishing meant a spinning rod, multiplier reel, and a Devon Minnow or Toby spoon. Today, due almost exclusively to tackle improvements, many salmon fishermen have put their spinning gear into semi-retirement. The only time that it might be brought out is for fishing an enormously wide river such as the Tay, where sheer casting range can be all-important, or on those days when the fly fisherman is beaten by a gale howling straight into his face.

This changeover from spinning to fly can, at one level, be seen as a more sporting attitude emerging, of men fishing for the fun of the thing and taking a pride in their skill at handling cold water tackle effectively. It takes good instruction, then plenty of dedicated practice. Yes, it is all these things but – a very important point – it is something more. The fact of the matter is that many, many salmon fishermen, myself included, have discovered that, with skilled handling, the cold water salmon fly will not only equal but actually better the spinner over the course of a season. At the risk of sounding pedantic and perhaps a little impolite, I shall state my opinion that, as

Spinning the Somerley Water at Ibsley on the Hampshire Avon

a casting and fishing instructor, I can teach a man enough to catch a salmon in half an hour with a spinning rod but, starting from scratch, it will take far longer to teach the skills of fly casting and presentation. Acknowledging that the spinner will perhaps catch his first salmon sooner, over the coming seasons the fly fisher will enjoy a greater level of success. Any fool can catch a salmon on a spinner but the dedicated and skilled fly fisherman will catch considerably more over the years and on a variety of rivers.

If any accolades for success in cold water fly fishing are to be given, they should really go to those who championed the introduction of articulated flies, the scientists who developed plastic lines and the rod builders who saw the potential in modern synthetic materials to produce long rods, at a reasonable weight.

Looking closer at the fly which, at the end of the day, is at the sharp end of the fisherman's weaponry and upon which success so heavily depends, its history is an interesting one. Until recent times, we were only considering the merits of one classic pattern of fly against another. All of these, for cold water use, would be tied on big single hooks.

In the middle of the last century, salmon flies would be dressed with whatever materials were available from the local haberdasher's shop, gathered on walks through the fields, or collected from the quarry species found in the bags of shooting men of that era.

Scope, that intriguing Tweedside character and fisherman, described such flies in *Days and Nights of Salmon Fishing on the Tweed*. This book was published in 1843.

'Lady of Mertoun'. An early Tweed fly from the days before exotica were introduced to the fly dresser from the far flung corners of the Empire. Described by Scrope in 1843

What marvellous names were borne by these flies – Lady of Mertoun, Toppy and Michael Scott, the latter being a legendary wizard of the Eildon Hills near Melrose. And, as you would expect, the fly named after him was indeed blessed with magical properties. When it came to fishing for salmon, Scrope described the Michael Scott as 'a most killing wizard'.

Kinmont Willie is a fly that I would like to try. Willie was a famed Border riever from that period in history lasting for hundreds of years before the crowns of Scotland and England were united. Generation after generation of bloody fighting, when a raiding party might number a thousand mounted troopers: 'Ride, ride, over the border . . .', and the blue bonnets of the Scottish border families rode for three *centuries*. The Highland clans were betrayed by a leader's egotism and the military ineptitude of their commanders in three short *years*. And yet, who is it that history remembers?

Who was Meg, of the fly 'Meg wi' the Muckle Mou''? This fly might well have been named after Mons Meg, the enormous and ancient siege cannon now installed at Edinburgh Castle. This, indeed, is a 'Meg with a big mouth'. But why, then, have a fly named Meg in her Braws? Braws is a Scots description of best clothes, to be worn to the Kirk on Sundays. It is also a mark of quality for more general use. So, when your gillie has just landed a fine salmon for you, its deep flanks dipped in the silver of the oceans, and with long tailed lice still clinging to its flanks, you will understand when he says 'Mon, sicca braw fush', that he means, in the English tongue, 'Man, such a great salmon', for in Scotland there is but one fish and that is a salmon. Anything else is named. A trout is a trout and a sea trout a sea trout, but a salmon is a 'fush'.

Be that as it may, there may still be some who would like to take a look at this lady in her finery, even if contrarily they may decide to throw her into the river!

Meg in her Braws

Wings	Light brown, from the head of a bittern.
Head	Yellow wool.
Next the head	Mottled blue feather from a jay's wing.
Body	Brown wool mixed with bullock's hair.
Towards the end of the body	Green wool, next to that crimson wool.
Tail	Yellow wool.
Round the body	Gold twist; over that, cock's hackle, black at the roots and red at the points.

Modern fly dressers, besides noting the simple and readily available materials used at that time, will also see that the technical terms of fly dressing had not been introduced in 1843. 'Next the head' is used to describe the throat hackle; 'Towards the end of the body' is now called the butt and tag; 'Round the body' includes not only the tinsel rib, but also the palmered hackle which, in that colouration, would be described as a Greenwell.

Such flies caught plenty of salmon, and still could. Their popularity, however, faded with the rise of the British Empire in the latter part of the nineteenth century. Explorers and hunters were discovering exotic birds with beautiful plumage.

It has been said that Irish fly dressers were the first to recognise the potential of these new materials. George Kelson may have tried to claim the credit for the Thunder and Lightning, still deadly in a falling and clearing water, but it was undoubtedly an Irish pattern in use before Kelson was born. Interestingly, apart from the jungle cock cheeks, the rest of the materials involved were local, the wing being a simple affair of bronze mallard. Indeed, it would seem reasonable to suppose that the Thunder and Lightning, minus the jungle cock, was in use long before the introduction of exotica to our shores. But when those exotica arrived, the fly dressers certainly had a field day. They created perfect gems using their craftsmanship and artistry to the full.

And if the Irish can claim the credit for starting this trend, it cannot be denied that the Scots were very quick in catching up on the Irish lead. Many famous patterns are the product of Scots ingenuity and inventiveness. And, like Scrope's flies, there is often a tale behind their names. Take, for example, the Jock Scott. One gentlemanly explanation of how this world-famous salmon fly, perhaps the most famous and effective of all classic patterns, came to be named is as follows. Lord John Scott was travelling by steamer to Norway, where he planned to catch some mighty salmon. He was accompanied by his gillie, and the noble lord suggested that, in order to while away the passage, his servant should tie up some flies. This was done, and a new pattern of fly emerged which not only proved successful in Norway, but also showed its powers on their return to Scotland. Hence, because of Lord John Scott, the fly was named. Well, that's only true insofar as it goes. What it omits to

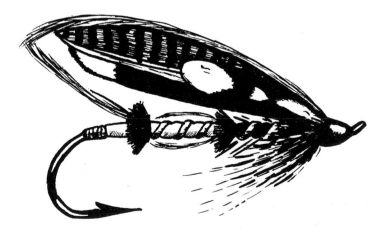

'Jock Scott'. Invented by Jock Scott, gillie to Lord John Scott, during a voyage to Norway, it quickly grew in popularity to become one of the best known, most used and most productive of classic, traditional salmon flies

mention is the gillie's name. Remember that Scottish society was based on a paternal rather than a feudal system. The gillie's name was no other than Jock Scott! Och well, many a record catch and fish was hooked by the gillie and landed by his gentleman! Just look at the materials used in this 'braw' fly:

Jock Scott

Tag	Round silver tinsel.
Tail	A topping and Indian crow.
Butt	Black ostrich herl.
Body	In two equal parts: the first half yellow floss, veiled above and below with toucan breast feathers. Then another black ostrich herl butt and the remaining half of black floss.
Ribs	Fine oval silver tinsel over the first half, broader oval tinsel over the second black half.
Body hackle	Black, over the black half of the body only.
Throat	Speckled gallena.
Wings	Two strips of dark, white-tipped turkey tails, back to back, then a mixed sheath of yellow, scarlet and blue swan, speckled bustard, florican bustard, golden pheasant tail, and two strands of peacock sword herl above. Then married narrow strips of teal and barred summer duck each side. Then bronze mallard as the final sheath. A golden pheasant topping over all.
Sides	Jungle cock.
Cheeks	Blue chatterer.
Head	Black varnish.

It is the wing of these classic patterns that is the greatest challenge to the fly dresser and, of all salmon wings, the Jock Scott's is perhaps the most difficult. Known as a 'built' wing, the three main sections of white-tipped turkey base, the 'mixed' wing and the final sheaths should overlap but not hide, like the slates on a roof.

The Jock Scott and a host of other patterns from the classic era are still in use today. Besides the Jock Scott, a list of those which continue to enjoy a measure of popularity includes names such as the Dusty Miller, Thunder and Lightning and Durham Ranger; silver-bodied flies such as the Yellow Torrish, Silver Doctor, Silver Wilkinson and, a great favourite, the Mar Lodge. Black-bodied flies have proved themselves ten thousand times over: Black Doctor and the Canadian tying of the Black Dose. And the Green Highlander earns its place still in some fly boxes, and there are many who would argue that more Atlantic salmon have fallen for a Blue Charm than any other pattern.

Yes, such flies still remain popular, particularly with American and Continental European anglers. In this country, however, it is rare to see them, although many gillies will privately, if not publicly, express their allegiance to such classic patterns. So, for the majority of British fishermen, what kind of fly has replaced the jewelled allure of these gems of salmon flies? It may not sound very impressive on paper but, if there is one fly of today that succeeds above all others in cold water conditions, it is the Willie Gunn.

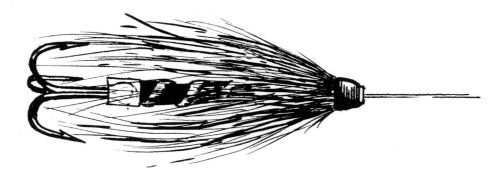

'Willie Gunn'. Compared to traditional flies, the dressing of the Willie Gunn tube fly is simple in the extreme – a gold ribbed, black body and a wing of mixed black, orange and yellow hair. But it is so successful in cold water conditions on many rivers that the spinner has been set aside in order to fish this fly

Body   Black floss or wool.
Rib   Oval gold.
Wing   Yellow under orange under black goat-hair or bucktail.

Simplicity itself, but fast earning the sort of reputation to make it the greatest cold water, British salmon fly of all time. Important as the pattern itself is, it is perhaps the actual design of fly which makes the Willie Gunn outstanding in terms of success. For this is one of the patterns closely connected with the modern generation of long articulated flies. Once the inherent problems involved with fishing a large single hook – its inability to hook and hold predictably – were overcome, the slim attractions of the articulates were discovered and then capitalised upon to the point where, in *Days and Nights of Game Fishing*, that great Scottish fisherman, Dr William B. Currie, could write of 'The Nearly Perfect Salmon Fly'.

More and more salmon fishermen on those beats which can produce salmon in cold water conditions are finding that they have virtually set aside the classic flies tied on single and double hooks. Today, they look no further than to tube flies, Waddingtons, and those flies that Bill Currie described – the wire-shanked flies that were developed by Rob Wilson of Brora. The problem some anglers found with the shank as designed by Richard Waddington was that it lacked weight and had a tendency to 'butterfly' in streamy water. The solution was simple. An already outstanding design was improved still further by slightly increasing the gauge and weight of wire used to make the shank. But let us not forget that it was Richard Waddington's original concept.

Waddington's philosophy on cold water salmon flies was set out in *Salmon Fishing*,

(Top) *The tradition in Scotland is for the long, double-handed salmon rod*

(Bottom) *Fine, streamy water to fish the fly, but the bankside trees necessitate the Spey casting techniques*

(Above) *A modern generation, simplified but highly effective salmon fly dressed by the author*

(Left) *A cane rod in action on the Dee. Today, most anglers choose carbon-fibre*

A summer salmon from the Spey, taken on a Munro Killer

published in 1959. He argued that the traditional salmon fly had been poorly served by the single hook. Besides the fact that, particularly in larger sizes fished in slacker water, the weight of metal in the bend and point of the hook would pull the fly off the horizontal, swimming in a down-tail position, there were better ways to represent the appearance of a small fish or eel-like creature which, we presume, is what the cold water flies are taken for. And so he designed his Waddington shank, which was, in its basic form, the shank of an ordinary salmon hook, but with the bend and point replaced by a small ring, to which a treble hook was to be attached. Originally, these shanks were dressed with conventional patterns, and they were dressed and marketed by Martins of Glasgow as 'Waddington Elverine Lures'.

Today, the dressing of Waddington shanks has, on the whole, gone over to the modern generation of simplified hair-wing patterns, with the long trailing hackles of Waddington's originals being replaced with goat or buck tail.

Then came the double-Waddington shank. In this design, a thinner gauge of wire was used for the shank, but doubled back to produce, as it were, a continuous closed loop, broken only at a point a little above the tail loop, in order to allow a treble hook to be attached or replaced. It was from this double-Waddington design that the Brora style of wire-bodied fly was developed. Various gauges of stainless steel wire were used by Rob Wilson to give the fisherman a choice of weight ranging from quite light to very heavy in a range of sizes. The popularity of this style of fly quickly spread from the Highlands and, with it, the new generation of cold water salmon flies like the legendary Willie Gunn, Sunrise, Sunset, Pilkington, and so on.

Whatever the popularity of Waddington and Brora-style flies with many knowledgeable Scottish gillies and fishermen, there can be little doubt that the majority of early spring and autumn salmon are still taken on tube flies. They became popular at about the same time as the early Waddingtons, at the start of the sixties. They are a simple and very effective design comprising a thinnish tube, through which the leader is threaded, and then tied to a treble hook. Their value was greatly increased by refinements such as an extension tube to hold the treble in line with the tubed shank. And their adaptability to a wide range of fishing situations and water depths was greatly enhanced by the variety of materials on offer: lightweight plastic, aluminium, copper and heavyweight brass tubes.

Talking of heavyweight brass tubes and, indeed, the heavier class of wire-bodied flies, leads to an interesting tactical point. Many experienced salmon fishermen now feel that this type of fly, certainly those in the 'super-heavy' class, is not really necessary. Indeed, many gillies on great salmon beats have a strong objection to already heavy tubes being wrapped with lead wire, or adorned with lead heads. Allied to an ultra-fast sinking line, such flies are often regarded as nothing more than a thin veil for the activities of a 'sniggler', the sort of man who doesn't really care where he hooks a salmon, be it in the mouth, back or flank. Our increasing experience of fishing the sunk fly shows that salmon, whilst not being as active in cold as in warm water, will still rise to take a fly. The whole question of depth is relative and, in most cold water salmon fishing situations, all that is required is a sinking line such as the

February on Beat 2 Lower of the Helmsdale – a time for fishing deep and slow with large flies

Wetcel 2 and a medium-weight fly, be it an aluminium or standard brass or copper tube, or wire-bodied design.

Incidentally, the dependence of these flies upon the use of treble hooks is interesting. In North America, such hooks are banned for the catching of Atlantic salmon. In this country we depend on them heavily throughout the season, and almost exclusively in cold water times. We applaud them as the most efficient of hookers and holders. The Americans, it seems, ban them for the same reason!

It is, perhaps, ironic that two of the greatest criticisms made by contemporary American outdoor writers and fishermen are, at one level, that we continue to spin for salmon and, at another, that we use tubes armed with trebles for cold water fishing. The fact of the matter is that they have no native equivalent of our salmon fishing outside the time of summer salmon and grilse and, in criticising spinning and the tube fly in one and the same breath, fail to recognise that it is the tube fly and the treble which, together with other advances in tackle, are making the spinning rod redundant on many British rivers.

Many British salmon fishermen would regard the changeover from classic traditional patterns tied on enormous single hooks, nick-named 'meat-hooks', to articulated flies armed with trebles as the greatest individual advance in the development of the salmon fly. Their use, allied to other developments in tackle, has made fly fishing a real proposition in even the heaviest of fishable cold water conditions and situations. Without these advances, the majority of those fishing the great beats would revert to the spinning rod for most of their cold water fishing. At a time when more and more fishermen are showing their willingness to accept the rewards of using fly tackle to maximum effect and advantage, any criticism of the articulated fly, other than the super heavies, should be put firmly in its place in regard to British fishing, and that place is in the waste paper basket.

In addition to the early sixties seeing the growing popularity of articulated flies, this was the time when plastic lines, rather than silk, took off in a big way. Perhaps the lion's share of attention has been given to the convenience of modern floating lines but, equally, the introduction of a full range of plastic sinkers has revolutionised our effectiveness in fishing the sinking line. As mentioned earlier, a line such as the Wetcel 2 will meet most needs, but we can also choose from a full range running from intermediates and neutral densities which just settle into the upper layer of streamy water, right through to high speed and ultra fasts, not to mention sink tips, with a floating mainline. The result is that the salmon fisherman, armed with a selection of these lines, is never again faced with a situation where he cannot fish his fly literally to whatever depth he chooses. In purely tactical terms, the range of modern plastic sinking lines is of inestimable value.

Finally, modern salmon fishermen owe an enormous debt to the pioneering work of rod designers and manufacturers. Again, we go back to the sixties when the firm of Bruce & Walker manufactured the first British prototype carbon-fibre rod. The history of this firm, which had already done so much for fibre-glass, is one of a search for perfection. It took some time to perfect the carbon rod but, by the mid to late seventies, practically all salmon fishermen were using them, and Jim Bruce and Ken Walker had firmly established themselves at the forefront of the market. Nor did it end there. In recent years, Bruce & Walker introduced the Hexagraph rod where flat carbon strips are laid on an ultra-light but solid core material. These rods were found to combine all the best of cane design, which they closely resemble, with the undoubted advantages of carbon-fibre in regard to weight saving. For me today, although I also use 16 and 17ft tubular carbon rods, pride of place for fishing the sinking line goes to my 15ft Walker Hexagraph. More and more British salmon fishermen are finding the advantages inherent in a rod of this type. Because of them, and long rods in general, further changes in fly line design had to be made.

Until the introduction of carbon-fibre rods, there was no need for a longer fly line than the standard 30 yards or, in the case of some manufacturers, slightly less. However, carbon-fibre means that longer rods can be comfortably used. As a rough rule of thumb, each extra foot of length on a double-handed salmon rod can be said to add about 3 yards in sheer casting range. Thus, a good caster who can put out 27 yards with a 14ft rod may well find he can cast 30 with a 15 footer, 33 with a 16 footer and 36 with a 17 footer. With a favourable breeze, these casting ranges can be extended. These ranges are associated with Spey casting, to which carbon rods have proved themselves ideally suited, where only a minimum of line needs to be shot.

Spey casting requires that none of the back tapered portion of a double-taper line should be outside the rod tip. Therefore, with a 15ft rod, unless shooting at least some line, there would have to be one or two turns of the mainline still on the reel. This gave a perfectly adequate length of line, about 25 yards for rather better than average casters but, for those with more experience and particularly when using longer rods, the standard line was just a touch inadequate for their needs. Hardy's were one of the first to produce a 40yd floating line, and Masterline produced 35yd salmon lines, sinkers as well as floaters. I have used Scientific Angler's lines since I was a boy, and was upset that they were, in this one aspect, appearing to lag behind, and I told them so. I thought that I was being ignored until earlier this year, at the start of 1989, when I got word that I could take delivery of an Aircel, Neutral Density and Wetcel 2, not in 35, not in 40, but in 42yd lengths!

Well, maybe 42 yards is pushing the boat out a bit, but better too much than too little. These lines will now become my standard armour, allied to articulated flies and the longer class of double-handed rods for fishing great beats on classic salmon rivers of a certain width, like the Spey, Tay and Tweed, where sheer casting range becomes paramount.

As mentioned earlier, the late Major the Hon. John Ashley Cooper was undoubtedly the most successful and experienced salmon fisherman of modern times. Here is what he had to say on rods and casting in relation to the great rivers, taken from *A Line on Salmon* published in 1983.

Having discussed rod weight, and stating that a 17ft carbon rod weighs less than a 14ft split cane, he continues:

> The longer the rod . . . the longer the cast that can comfortably be made; and on a big river or even a medium one the ability to throw a long line whenever wanted is invaluable. Thirty-five yards is none too long a distance to be aimed at . . . .

And he then goes on to state his belief that most fishermen handicap themselves by using rods of a maximum length of 14ft, incapable of achieving such a range. Of course we cannot all be Ashley Coopers but, in defining the true road to success in big river fishing which comes down to effective casting range and water command, he gives the dedicated visitor to great beats on classic rivers a target to aim for.

Incidentally, you will still find some writers, who really should know better, saying

'Gold Riach'. A traditional Spey fly of ancient lineage, it was described by Knox in 1872. The long, flowing hackle, taken either from a Spey Cock or a heron, works in a lifelike manner in the water, and one suspects from the Gold Riach's profile that it might be taken for a shrimp or prawn

that the Spey cast can only be done with a floater. This is nonsense. If they said that it is only possible to Spey cast a line that is on the surface, that would be a different matter. Prior to the Spey cast, usually a double Spey with a sinking line, the sunk line must be rolled up to the surface, from where it can be lifted and thrown with ease. Indeed, many experienced fishermen find that, because of its thinner diameter for a given weight, which helps to cut through any contrary breeze, the sinking line is, if anything, more effective than a floater. If, on the other hand, you use a sinking, shooting head, be aware that you might just as well use a stiff fibre-glass rod, and nine out of ten gillies will think, if not say, that you might just as well get out the spinning rod. 'Och, I don't know what yon man thinks he is doing, but it certainly isn't fly fishing'; so there we are.

To summarise this section on cold water fishing: it would be hard to overestimate the changes in attitudes as well as techniques in early spring and autumn salmon fishing brought about through increased casting range and effective water command by longer carbon rods, modern plastic lines and the great resurgence of interest in Spey casting. Ally these to the excellent hooking and holding potential of articulated flies armed with treble hooks, and you get a formidable combination that, for at least half of the British salmon season, has transformed fly fishing on many beats.

CHAPTER 6

SPRING AND SUMMER FISHING

According to most accounts, there was very little low water, summer salmon fishing, as we know it today, being practised before the start of this century. Perhaps one of the reasons for this was that there was nothing like the same pressure on salmon fisheries. Anglers could pick and choose their times and, therefore, outside the high and cold water periods of early spring and autumn, nobody would bother to wet a line except at such times as fresh fish had entered their beat on the tail of a spate, when large flies fished on sinking lines would still prove effective. Those gentlemen and gillies who would go to the trouble of tempting salmon in warm water with sea trout-sized flies were quite exceptional, but they were pointing the way towards the development of late spring and summer tactics by showing that, at this time of the season, salmon can be tempted to take if offered a relatively small fly.

The idea that salmon were interested usually by a relatively small fly once the water temperature had risen above 50 degrees did not really catch on until the early years of this century and, with it, dawned the realisation that these smaller flies should be fished close to the water's surface in order to achieve the best results. This factor, this degree of realisation, served to transform the pattern of fishing on great beats where, previously, summer fish might only have been tried for with a natural bait.

What would prove to be the best tackle and tactics to present small flies close to the surface? This was a question that vexed turn-of-the-century fishermen. The development of successful warm water tactics was a gradual process, but it can be considered as very largely due to the fishing experiences of three individuals: Arthur Wood of Cairnton, 'the father of greased-line fishing'; Alexander Grant, known as 'The Wizard of the Ness', and Percy Laming, a great fisherman of the northern rivers.

Of the three, Arthur Wood is undoubtedly the best known, but he is also one of the most ill-represented fishermen of the past. Enormously popular, he had to suffer the fate of seeing his peculiarly individual technique subjected to numerous inter-pretations, few of which might have been in accord with his own ideas on the subject. Wood perhaps also suffered from the problem of finding it hard to describe in words exactly what he was achieving in practice. But that is enough of judging the man and his disciples. Let us rather concentrate on the technique which he popularised so widely.

Time to try the floating line on the Hampshire Avon at Bisterne

ARTHUR WOOD

A. H. E. Wood of Cairnton has been described as the father of greased-line fishing. As you will probably know, greasing lines became a thing of the past with the introduction of modern, plastic floating lines but, prior to that, silk lines were the fly fisherman's standard armour and, if he wanted them to float, then he had to grease them. Wood cannot, however, be considered the true father of the floating line because lines had been greased for this purpose long before he put in an appearance. Nevertheless, he certainly developed a technique of fishing with the floating line that was unique and immediately became very popular.

Wood's thinking and methods are described in *Greased Line Fishing for Salmon* by Jock Scott. How good a book is it? Often, when a third party is describing the ideas of another and how they perform in practice, the reader has the benefit of an objective viewpoint. But somehow, in his book, Jock Scott misses the mark. It is as if he is merely repeating phrases and ideas that he has heard from the mouth of Wood, rather than offering any sort of a practical appraisal. Therefore, because Wood seemed bent on drawing from his southern chalk-stream experience, the book is full of descriptions of moths fluttering over the water, likening the technique to 'nymph fishing for salmon', and a near obsession with the need to avoid drag when, as any practical fisherman can see, the technique actually relies on drag in order to fish the fly attractively. What Wood really discovered was a means of fishing the fly so that its lateral movement as it swims across the stream is under the fisherman's control. The fly can virtually be made to hang in one spot, hovering enticingly in streamy water, or its lateral movement can be accelerated to fish across slower water. The technique involved little more than the judicious use of upstream or downstream mends. But why bother?

The reasons lie in the thinking behind our choice of fly for summer use. In cold water conditions, it seems reasonably safe to say that we are trying to give some sort of impression of a small fish which the salmon may associate with its feeding experience in water temperatures of less than 50 degrees. Most of the time, when we fish such flies and particularly when the water temperature is not far above freezing point, we fish them deep. But then come warmer water temperatures and, once the temperature has steadied at over 50 degrees, fishing experience reveals that, by and large, salmon are more likely to show a greater interest in a relatively small fly, fished just below the surface. What could these small flies be said to represent?

One theory is that the small, drab flies that we so often use in summer may trigger off a reaction due to their caricature of the insects that the salmon was used to feeding on in its immature time in freshwater. Another is that the smaller flies may represent shrimp and other invertebrates that the salmon fed on while at sea, perhaps in warmer ocean currents, thus accounting for the change of interest according to temperature. Certainly the various patterns of Shrimp Fly can be very productive during the floating line time of the season, usually from mid-May until the back end of September.

A fine salmon taken on a floating line and small fly

It has to be said that some fishermen, perhaps wisely, prefer to go no further than stating that what we are representing is a stimulus, small in size, that has a fair chance of triggering off the desired response from a salmon – it takes the object into its mouth. After it has done that, it may seem nothing more than academic whether its response was out of a conditioned feeding reflex or from curiosity, anger, fear or whatever.

Whatever our thoughts may be on the subject, we shall probably accept that our offering should fish in as natural a way as possible. All our possibilities come down to one common denominator, and it is that our relatively small summer flies represent some small creature and, in accepting that, we acknowledge that there must be severe limitations on the water speed of the fly. In a strong stream, a creature barely one inch in length could hardly hold its own. It certainly would not be capable of darting forward into the force of the current and, therefore, we must fish it as slowly as possible, literally hanging in the stream.

Looking deeper into Wood's technique, the stumbling block for many fishermen who might otherwise adopt his style more fully would appear to concern the question of drag, and how it is to be interpreted. As already stated, Wood had a tendency to talk in the language of the chalk streams and, on that basis, many of his disciples in the inter-war years misinterpreted what he was really trying to say. In fact, on studying Wood's words closely, it is quite apparent that the drag of which he spoke bore no resemblance to what the majority of those who fish the dry fly for trout would recognise as such.

As a writer, I know that people will often convince themselves that you have said something which is more a product of what they want to hear, or which suits their own particular purpose. For example, in a recent issue of a contemporary magazine, I was taken to task on the 'Readers' Letters' page for feeding slack line to a taking fish. My reaction was not so much one of anger as of amusement, because a few pages further on there was one of my own articles which stated, as I always have done, that in no circumstances do I ever feed slack line to a taking salmon! Still, I suppose this is just one of those things we have to accept.

But knowing it, let's take a close look at what Wood actually said himself, and then read it again and again until the words are etched on our memory.

> With the greased line, you are able to control the position and angle of the fly in the water and also, to a very great extent, the speed at which it travels.
>   I cast rather more upstream than the orthodox cast of a salmon fisherman, then lift my line off the water and, without moving the fly, turn over a loop of line upstream and across to prevent any drag on the fly.

There, in a nutshell, we have the philosophy of Wood's technique. And yet, what a host of misinterpretations it has been subjected to, time after time after time. Surely, what Wood is saying is that a floating line allows us to control the speed of the fly, and when he is talking about drag he speaks only of lateral movement – a method to avoid the fly being dragged across the stream when, if the line is not mended, a downstream belly is formed. And he did not say that he cast upstream at all, only that he cast rather more upstream than the standard cast of his contemporaries.

Wood's casting angle needs a little more attention. Standard practice in those days was to cast at an angle of no more than 45 degrees to the bank. This figure is still widely advocated today. Looking at original diagrams of Wood's technique, it is apparent that he normally cast at an angle of something like 70–80 degrees to the stream, only slightly downstream from straight across, but downstream nevertheless.

It is now that we enter into something of a 'Which came first, the chicken or the egg?' situation. Wood may well have adopted this casting angle, at least originally, for a reason that had little to do with practical fishing technique. We suggest that he simply had to cast at this angle in order to cover fish lying far out from the bank because, as contemporary photographs show, Arthur Wood may not have seen getting his feet wet as part of the joys of the salmon fishing experience. You look at these pictures and see a big man, often with a cigar, and wearing a tweed suit with stockings and stout leather shoes. But which came first; did he cast square because he could avoid wading or did he not wade because he could see no need for it? And, at the end of the day, does it really matter because, chicken or egg, Wood's success showed all the rest of us that it was possible to cast fairly square and, so long as we mend line, to fish the fly slowly enough across the stream for it to appear natural.

> The lifting-over of line is done to correct a fault, namely, to take the downstream belly out of a line and thus relieve the pull or pressure of the current on the line, which is communicated to the fly and exhibits itself as drag.

And he goes on to state that the purpose of mending is solely to 'prevent drag or, more often, to control the speed of the fly across the river'.

This ability to control the speed of the fly across the river was *the* major achievement involved in Arthur Wood's greased-line technique.

Some writers have maintained that the method involved fishing an almost lifeless fly, broadside to and at the whim of the current. *It did not.* What it was all about was fishing a fly as slowly as possible which, for much of the time in salmon fishing, is exactly the required presentation.

Think of what the fly is doing as it swims across a stream. Let us say that the current is running at 4mph. That will be the water speed of a fly held stationary, on the dangle, in the stream. Immediately that fly starts to swim sideways, its water speed increases. With a knowledge of vectors, we can work out the resolved water speed. It is done by triangulation and, for example, remembering the 3, 4, 5 triangle from school-room days, we can state that a fly swimming into a 3mph current and crossing it at 4mph will have a resolved water speed of 5mph.

The purpose of the upstream mend is to move the point on which the line swings further out across the stream. Think of the line as a pendulum. Move the point of the pendulum out by putting a big upstream mend into the line, and you are

Late spring on the Spey with salmon running through a pool

effectively fishing the fly on the dangle and minimising resolved water speed by restricting the speed of the fly swimming across the current.

This is only a brief consideration of Wood's technique but, before leaving it, perhaps it is worth emphasising that his technique was concerned solely with controlling the speed of the fly, which is not quite the same as suggesting that his purpose was always to reduce the fly's speed. There were occasions when he sought to increase the speed. The need for this occurs in slackish water; for example, when a fly has been fished across a strong stream and eventually emerges into the slack water at its cheek. Here Wood states: 'If the fly hardly moves and begins to sink, draw in line with your fingers very slowly and keep the fly as near the surface as you can.' It is this control of the speed of the fly swimming across the current which is the basis of Wood's technique, and an invaluable addition to the salmon fisherman's technique, for which he should be remembered.

Any discussion of the rods he used or the hooks he favoured is little more than a smoke screen hiding the truth of what we owe to this great fisherman. I readily admit that in the past, I have been guilty of denigrating the man, but I shall do it no more. Any of us, each and every time we thrown an upstream mend into our fly lines to fish the fly that little bit more tantalisingly, causing it to hover and shimmer across the salmon's field of view, should say a silent prayer to the memory of A. H. E. Wood of Cairnton on the Aberdeenshire Dee.

There is, of course, another method of controlling the speed of the fly. Less positive than Wood's technique, perhaps, but the method of warm water fishing about to be described could be said to have provided the basis of modern salmon fishing tactics.

ALEXANDER GRANT

As was made clear in the previous section of this chapter, the modern salmon angler owes a great deal to Arthur Wood. However, the devotion shown to Wood by his contemporaries denied them any real consideration of the thoughts, tackle and technique of another great slayer of fish, namely Alexander Grant. Many modern anglers use what they believe to be a new style of technique which, in reality, Grant was using at the turn of the century.

The reasons for Wood receiving more than his fair share of attention are simple. He was in a position to invite the famous and influential to fish his beat, Cairnton, on the Aberdeenshire Dee. He was a sociable man and entertained on a lavish scale. Equally, many salmon fishermen of the time – the earlier part of this century – were gentlemen from the South of England. Naturally, these men spent a large part of their fishing season on their native chalk streams. Mr Wood's descriptions of 'the elimination of drag' and 'nymph fishing for salmon,' were in a language and about an experience with which they could identify. And they were attracted to a technique which suggested they could employ shorter, lighter and more handy rods, maintaining fishing range by presenting their fly more squarely to the stream.

Alexander Grant, on the other hand, was a native Highlander who shunned publicity. This is quite typical of his race. One day, Grant was casting on the Ness and giving some instruction to Lord Zetland. An elderly inhabitant of Inverness was walking by and seeing the enormous length of line which Grant was famed for handling rolling out cleanly above the water, he cried out, without breaking step, 'My gosh, what a throw! Tell him naething; tell him naething!'

Grant was of deceptively small stature. He packed an awful lot of power into his short body. His muscles had been built swinging a felling axe in the years of his youth. He was able to use long, heavy greenheart rods with relative ease.

His casting technique, the switch cast, virtually indistinguishable from the modern single-Spey, was practically unique in its effectiveness. And this was no mere circus trick. Jock Scott, one of the best known commentators on salmon fishing in his time, described Grant frequently hooking fish in high water with a huge 4/0 double iron at ranges up to 50 yards, and with both hooks right home over the barbs.

The real parting of the ways between Wood and Grant was that Wood's technique was totally dependent upon fishing with a floating line. Grant would have none of this. His technique was christened the 'oiled-line technique'. You grease a silk line to make it float, but apply oil if you wish it to sink. Jock Scott described Grant's aversion to the floating line in a book titled *Fine and Far Off*.

'Now', says Mr Grant, 'is a fish an idiot to stand this sort of thing? I know very well that tons of fish have been and are killed in this way but might not far more have been killed if all this surface glitter were avoided? Some fish don't mind it, others do; it depends on the angle of the light to the line, as to whether it sparkles or not. You are, in effect, scratching the surface of the water, and if you are unlucky enough to get the line at just the right angle to the sun's rays, that line is going to be encased in a glittering halo of minute bubbles and ripples, millions of them, and each one a mirror.

Then there were Grant's opinions on the vision of fish. Many suggest that fish have limited vision. To Grant, this idea was quite simply rubbish, certainly as regards their vision of anything in or on the water. Anybody who has witnessed a salmon racing for many yards through the water to take a fly will not hesitate to join in with Grant's opposition. Only last season, I was fishing down a fine pool, my fly swinging nicely across the tail of the glide, when I felt a light pluck at my fly, nothing more. I decided to try out the suggestion that it is best to rest the fish for a few minutes before presenting the fly once more. I simply pulled in some line, perhaps ten yards in all, and left the fly hanging on the dangle. After a minute or two, and intending to give the salmon considerably longer, I re-cast the short line, for want of something better to do. As the fly swam across, I saw a shape coming up from the tail like a torpedo, bulging the surface and taking the fly with a real bang. That was one salmon, at least, who didn't seem to be suffering any limits to vision. Incidentally, the fly involved was a little wisp of a Shrimp Fly on a size 10 double.

It was for this and other reasons that Grant developed his own style of warm water

The Oykel – a wild and spectacular salmon river for excellent spring and summer sport

fishing, presenting the fly 'fine and far off'. He agreed with Wood that, in summer water and temperatures, salmon were most likely to take a relatively small fly fished close to the surface. It was his solution as to how this presentation should be best achieved, in his case with a sinking line, which was so radically different from the technique of Wood.

Floating or sinking line? Grant had a saying: 'You don't believe me, eh? Come on down to the river and I'll show you.' Well, I was never able to go to the river with him, but I have been able to take his teachings and, my goodness, they do work.

Alexander Grant's technique involved using a sinking line, regardless of water temperature and season. In order to be effective, the fisherman must be able to cast as long a line as possible. The salmon are literally left to hook themselves.

Remember, you cannot really mend the sinking line, certainly not when it has cut below the surface. Therefore, the technique depends, in order to control the speed at which the fly swims across the stream, on casting a long line at a fairly shallow,

Happy to pose with a fine July salmon from the Aboyne Water of the Dee

downstream angle. The fly swims across slowly at the end of the line acting like a pendulum. The longer the cast and the steeper the downstream angle, the slower the fly comes across. Grant himself seldom cast at a greater angle than 35 degrees to the bank and, in fast water, he would reduce this to below 20 degrees – practically straight back downstream.

Grant's method of hooking salmon attracted to his hovering fly is closely linked to the reasons why, even on a sinking line, he could fish his small fly close to the surface. He used a square-plait, single-taper line. The heaviest portion of the line, closest to the rod, would sink the fastest, and the thin tip would ride high in the water. The line would, in effect, adopt a long drawn-out, upward-sweeping curve in the water. Today, we would fish an intermediate or neutral density line.

Besides the fact that this allows the small fly to fish up to the surface, it automatically creates a form of 'cushion' to the pull of a taking fish. The long curve would straighten, giving the salmon scope to hook itself and, by the time Grant actually felt his fish, transmitted as a long slow draw on the line, it had already hooked itself. Simple, but very effective.

As already stated, Grant's technique was to fish 'fine and far off', his object being to reduce any possibility of alarming a fish. It should be noted that he never said the floating line would not catch salmon, only that it would put down some that might otherwise have been potential takers. As he said: 'No fish would like to see a big, black snake floating over his head – and the line would look dark to a fish looking up at it against the light'. His aim was to fish the fly with the absolute minimum of disturbance, in such a way that it should be very easy to take at a slow and easy pace.

He used long rods, principally to increase his casting range and water coverage, and very finely tapered silk sinking lines. As described in Jock Scott's book, the object of this very fine taper is to:

a. . . . put the small fly in very quietly and gently, without the vestige of a splash;
b. to swim near the surface in the slow stream, and
c. to be as invisible as possible to the fish.

Grant did not believe in shooting line. In fact, it made him swear: '.........!' he yells, 'are you trying to spin?'

He got in well upstream of the fish, and cast a straight line down to them, at a relatively shallow angle because a fly, presented in this fashion, will swim very slowly. . Unlike Wood, Grant was never keen on the single hook for salmon. He firmly believed in the double hook, and few today would argue with his tastes for a nice bend, not too wide, small barbs set near the point, and a turned-up eye.

Grant and Wood; Wood or Grant; which one of them was right? The truth of the matter is that they both were! But not all of the time and not in all places. Modern summer salmon fishing techniques are, in reality, a combination of what was best from both men's techniques. Before we leave fishermen of the past, however, there is one other fisherman of this century to be considered, and he is Percy Laming.

PERCY LAMING

The name of Percy Laming may not be widely known in salmon fishing circles. He was, however, a great fisherman, particularly on the Aberdeenshire Dee, in the days before Arthur Wood came on to the scene. Laming killed an approximate total of 4,500 salmon in his fishing career. He enjoyed single day takes of 21, 19, 17 and, on two occasions, 15 salmon in a day. These figures clearly show the level of his experience. He was a man who refused to be stereotyped into a set approach. And what he himself found was that, while the 'slow fly – no drag' techniques akin to Wood's and Grant's took a good share of the fish, there were times when drag, if used constructively, could tempt the otherwise untemptable.

Laming believed, and proved, that a fly that is dragging downstream will move and attract fish. Knowing where a fish was, or was likely to be, Laming would cast square across to land his fly immediately upstream of its position. The fast central current would immediately catch the line, bellying it downstream, and pulling the fly after it, whipping it across the salmon's field of vision. It could be said that he was the inventor of the sink tip line because he greased all but the last two yards of his silk line. He used flies with some flash about them, tied on double hooks, normally a size 8 or 6, and this technique, which came to be termed 'controlled drag', he used most productively in low warm water.

Laming was insistent that this was a technique in its own right and should be fished as such, rather than simply providing an excuse for a squarer cast than standard practice. Its user should be thinking hard about what he is trying to achieve. This type of stimulus seems to evoke a swift predatory response from salmon when it works, and one is reminded of grilse turning to chase and grab a tiny spinner, cast upstream and brought back over their lie. Takes are positive, even savage. Laming discovered that it was possible to fish the fly too quickly but, normally, he found that the general rule was 'the faster the better'.

If this seems to be in direct opposition to Wood and Grant, it must be remembered that, with this form of controlled drag, the fly should be heading downstream as it passes the salmon. This is very important. The current may be moving at 4mph. Therefore, fishing in the downstream style, the fly, if swimming head into the current on the dangle, has a water speed of 4mph. Now, to achieve that same water speed when swimming downstream, it must be swimming at 4mph in excess of the water current or, in other words, at a downstream speed of 4mph relative to the current, but at 8mph relative to the river bed and bank. Let's not forget that small creatures can swim downstream as well as up.

Laming's method, therefore, involves whipping a fairly large, flashy fly across the salmon's vision, without giving the fish time to make a close inspection. If the fish is aroused, it responds by immediate pursuit.

There is, however, a very real and valid objection to the use of this method. When used in unscrupulous hands in times of low water, it is far too likely to lead to the foul hooking of fish, particularly where they are concentrated in pools. It is, therefore, a method only to be used in the right place and at the right time. But it does provide fishermen with a very important lesson as to the behaviour of salmon where, as one modern writer has said, there is no room for the words 'always' or 'never'.

MODERN TIMES

This discussion of fishermen of the past, and their solutions to fishing a small fly close to the surface, should have revealed that, besides size and depth, fishing technique is deeply concerned with controlling the speed of lateral movement of the fly, the rate at which it swims across the river. Laming's technique is certainly worthy of note and therefore deserves inclusion, but it is Wood and Grant who were the real fathers of modern warm water fishing. Do we still think that controlling the water speed of the fly is so very important?

As mentioned many times in this book, the late Major the Hon. John Ashley Cooper still stands head and shoulders above the throng of modern fishermen. Nobody could rival his skill, knowledge and experience. Even in his passing a short time ago, he remained the greatest fisherman of modern times. After a day on one of the Norwegian rivers that he loved, he enjoyed good company and dinner before making his way to bed. He never awoke. Most would agree that he could not have found a more fitting finale.

I remember asking him his opinion on controlling fly speed. He believed very strongly that it was the most important aspect of salmon fishing, and he stated that the fisherman who controls the speed of the fly, rather than leaving it all to the current, will catch two or even three times as many fish.

This control extends not only to fishing a fly as slowly as possible as it comes across streamy water, but also to accelerating it as it enters the slack.

Bearing in mind this point about fly control, it might be said that, whereas developments in modern tackle have radically transformed the face of cold water fishing, the changes in warm water fishing are not so obvious. They are there, however, and even if fairly subtle in the shift of emphasis, can be clearly recognised.

There has been a move away from the teaching of Wood and his disciples. The basic technique of modern summer tactics is much more akin to the technique of Alexander Grant, and his 'fine and far off' approach.

Arthur Wood popularised the double-handed 12ft rod as the tool for warm water fishing. Even when cane gave way to fibre-glass, this remained the popular length. Rods of 14ft were still considered fairly cumbersome tools to be kept in reserve for whatever cold water fly fishing might be done. The situation since the advent of carbon-fibre has been a branching out towards the two extremes of length. Today, on British rivers, you will see all manner of rod lengths being used for summer salmon fishing, from mighty 17 and 18 footers to relatively minute single-handed 9 footers. First, let us take a look at the long rods.

On a river the size of the Tay, most gillies will consider you a bit light in the upper storey just for proposing to fish the fly in cold water conditions. Their river, they argue, is simply too massive to be covered adequately by a fly rod. However, come the summer, when the Tay shrinks away to become, as it were, rivers within a river, the fly rod becomes a definite proposition. And yet you will still need to push casting range and water command out to their extremes. Some gillies on the Tay regard a 17 footer as a relatively short rod, and would choose an 18 or even 20ft pole. The advantages of such rods are set out in Chapter 5 of this book on Early Spring and Autumn Fishing, and will not be repeated here. These rods are long and supple and, with an 11 line, have sensitivity to fish flies down to size 8 or 10 on 12lb bs leaders. This is as small as we should ever need to go on the wide expanses of a middle or lower beat of a big river which, even when it is summer-shrunk, still manages to carry an enormous thrust of water.

Having said that, it has to be added that the Tay is, in sheer terms of size, the greatest challenge in these islands to the long-range caster. The Ness comes close but most rivers do not require anything like the casting range of 18 and 20ft rods. Rods of 16 and 17ft are popular on rivers like the Spey, to reach a potential of 35yd casts but, even so, the favourite choice will be a 15 footer. This length of rod is, to the salmon fisherman, what the 12-bore with 28in barrels is to the game shooter.

In this 15ft length, of course, it is possible to choose a wide range of rods in regard to their action. Some are quite steely and designed primarily for the rigours of sunk line work at the start and end of the season. Others are more sensitive and ideally suited to a finer summer technique, while still having the capability to throw 30yd of line in a Spey cast. True, it is nothing like the distance cast by Alexander Grant but, by combining his basic technique with the best of Wood's tactic, it is possible to achieve the same water coverage and fly control. This is done by casting at a rather wider angle than Grant would have deemed ideal but, by mending line in the manner of Wood, the fly speed is still controlled. We now accept what Grant believed all those years ago. However, we have all seen so many salmon killed on the floating line in this century, and find it so convenient for casting and handling, that we will not give it up.

This is not quite true. Other writers and fishermen besides myself have, in recent years, been describing our successes on the relatively new intermediate and neutral density lines. They do not suit everybody; far from it. Just one quick mend can be got in before the line settles into the water, so they put a greater reliance on casting ability in terms of sheer range in order to gain the same water coverage.

Many of those who have reverted to these ultra-slow sinking line techniques for warmer water fishing, have found the results to be well worth the little extra effort required. This, however, is a book on great salmon beats, and this chapter is on how the majority choose to fish them and so, for now, let's stick with the floating line! A floating line, long casting and mending, coupled with deep wading when the need arises – that is the modern approach to fishing a small fly close to the surface as used by the majority of salmon fishermen on the great beats of medium to large rivers.

On beats on smaller rivers, our summer salmon flies may be fished in very much the same way but because the need for long-range casting has gone, and because we

Dusk on the Spey – fishing Pollowick at an excellent time of day for summer sport

are fishing to specific areas rather than fishing long stretches of holding water, we can look to shorter rods for more accuracy and even greater sensitivity. When the summer sun blazes on a shrunken spate stream, and you are thinking of presenting a wisp of a fly on a light leader, there is no question about using a rod of 15ft or more, with an 11 or 12 line. For this style of fishing, some British fishermen will choose a single-handed rod of 10–11ft loaded with a 6 or 7 line for a sensitive approach to summer salmon and grilse. However, even in low water, and certainly when fishing chances are at their best following a freshet of rain, there are many real arguments for a double-handed 13 footer, particularly where the nature of the river banks requires any amount of roll and Spey casting. There is no need to sacrifice sensitivity to any great extent. My own 13 footer is best suited with an 8 line but will also handle a 7.

'Stoat's Tail'. One of the modern generation of summer flies, the Stoat's Tail has proved its worth on a host of salmon rivers. It could not be simpler, with its black hair wing, hackle and body broken only by a silver rib and perhaps a hint of yellow feather for a tail

Nevertheless, if mainly in the context of small river, low water fishing, it must further be acknowledged that on many medium-sized and even larger river beats, more and more British salmon fishermen are following the North American lead and seeking summer sport on single-handed rods. There are, however, subtle differences between the two approaches. Because the British still have their double-handed rods to use in partnership with the single, they have less need for very powerful singles, capable of throwing the necessarily heavy line to punch out, say, a size 4 double hook. It would probably be true to say of great beats in Britain that they are fished with the double-handed rod, in the main, until fishermen feel that a size 8 or less is the required medicine, and it is then that a few of them, rather than choosing one of the shorter double-handed rods, like the 13ft and 8 line combination described above, will opt for a single-handed of about 10ft with a 7 or 8 line. It can be argued that the choice of a single-handed rod does not allow the fisherman to reach full potential in terms of casting range and water command; nevertheless, the single could be said to be the better choice for sheer fun and sport. And fishing should be about having fun.

As more and more netting stations are bought out and a stop put to their activities, it is inevitable that many of our great beats will enjoy bonanzas of summer salmon and grilse. These will provide ever greater opportunities for the single-handed rod enthusiasts. If I were in the business of making predictions, my money would be on the probability of more and more of our sport being undertaken with the shorter rod, but only in the low water summer months.

Typical of the size of summer salmon and grilse: an 8-pounder

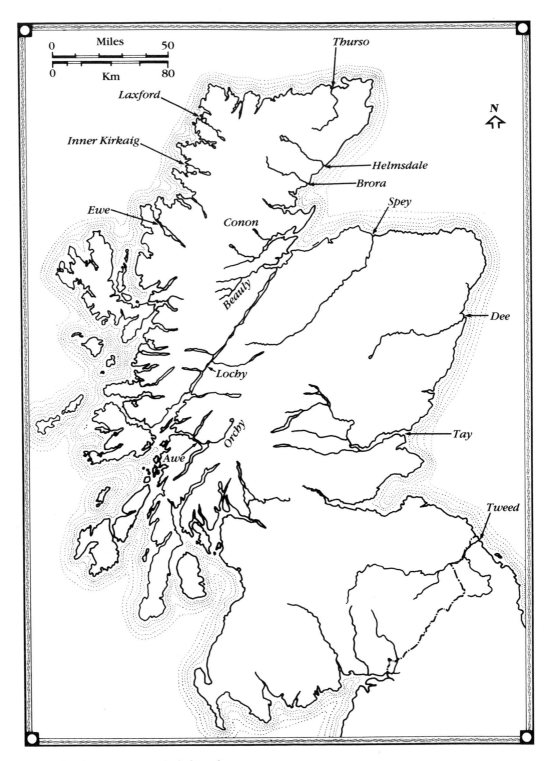

Scottish salmon rivers included in the text

THE
GREAT SALMON
BEATS

Lord Thurso enjoying his river with a young visitor

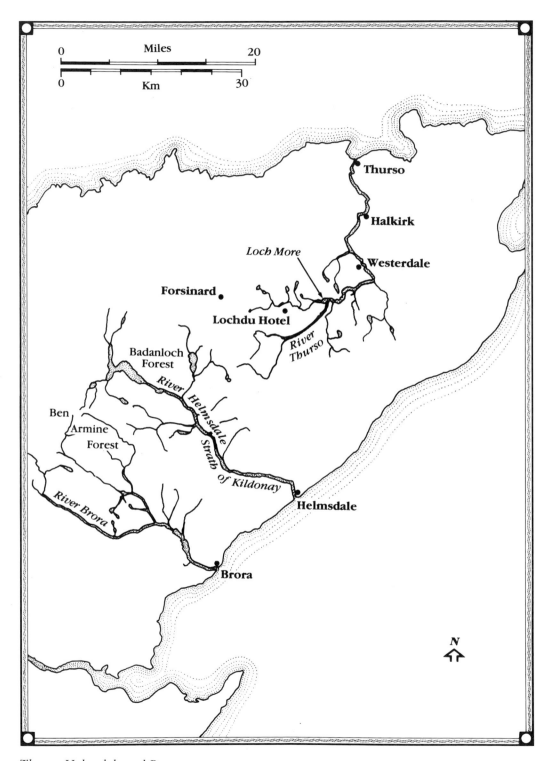

Thurso, Helmsdale and Brora

CHAPTER 7

THURSO, HELMSDALE AND BRORA

The Great Glen runs from Fort William on the west coast to Inverness on the east. The land lying to the north of it is both remote and dramatic. The high and rugged terrain of the West Highlands, with its relatively short and swift rivers, falls away towards the east coast, leading to a gentler landscape of coastal plains and flow country.

The rivers and beats of those rivers lying to the north-east of the Great Glen have a character practically of their own. These are fly-only rivers. Perhaps because of this, while standard salmon fly fishing techniques and tactics are employed, other more specialist techniques have also been developed.

Flowing through relatively flat country, it is inevitable that many pools, while undoubtedly holding salmon, lack the necessary current to fish the fly effectively. The highly original solution is the technique known as backing-up, where the fisherman starts casting at the tail of the pool and, by walking a few paces upstream and drawing in line by hand, literally swims the fly across the fish. To those whose experience goes no further than conventional fly tactics – starting at the head of the pool, allowing the water current to fish the fly round, then taking a pace or two downstream before casting again, and thus covering all the likely water – backing-up may seem highly improbable as a successful fishing tactic. However, salmon in these northern waters will sweep into the attack on a fly fished in this way. So much so that many fishermen, even on those pools with sufficient current to work the fly, will fish down the pool in the conventional way and, if no salmon has been obliging, immediately start to back-up the pool.

Strangely, perhaps, this technique of backing-up a pool does not seem to travel well from the place of its birth. It may work on some southern waters on occasion, but nowhere does it work so well as on the slower, sluggish pools of certain stretches of rivers in the far north-east.

Another local tactic, one that takes many a fish from rivers such as the Helmsdale, is dibbling. This involves fishing two flies on the leader, one being tied on a dropper some 3–4ft above the point fly. A long rod and short line aid the fisherman in fishing his pair of flies with the dropper cutting across the surface of streamy water, up in the throats and headstreams of holding pools. Salmon and grilse will rise to and take a fly fished in this manner, providing great excitement and sport. This tactic can be used on most Highland streams, although it never does great things on lowland rivers except from time to time, when the principal quarry is summertime grilse, lying in rough, broken water.

Another claim to fame of these rivers lying to the north-east of the Great Glen is that they are the home of a host of successful salmon fly patterns and designs. The Collie Dog, often little more than an aluminium tube to which has been whipped some long black hairs, originally cut from the hind-leg feathering of a Border Collie sheepdog, is but one north-eastern pattern to burst onto the salmon fishing scene and rewrite the rule books. The tremendously successful Willie Gunn, named after a local gillie, has virtually transformed experiences with the sunk line in cold water conditions for some people, and not only in the north-east.

In brief, these rivers of the north-east, the Thurso, Helmsdale and Brora, have produced not only hundreds of thousands of salmon for those who make the long journey to fish their beats, but also some of the Atlantic salmon world's most original techniques and tackle and a legacy of fishing lore and good sense that is almost inestimable in its value.

We shall deal here with the rivers and their beats by starting at the northernmost tip of the east coast. In fact, this river does not flow east at all. The flow is practically due north and it is, of course, the Thurso.

THE THURSO

Those who fish the Thurso in the County of Caithness claim that it is the best salmon river in the north. Well, there are certainly few rivers of its size that enjoy annual rod catches in excess of 1,000 fish.

As to its geography, the Thurso's source is at a height of 538m, being recognised as a spring on the windswept Knockfin heights. The upper part of its course is across deep peat-covered moorland, home to grouse and red deer, over the rocks of the Strathhalladale granite and gravel churned down by glaciers of the last Ice Age. The gravel is most significant. It provides the salmon with their spawning redds. Equally, this upper section of the river, together with its tributaries such as the Rumsdale and Sleach waters which, like the main river, are spring-fed, provides the nursery area of the river's young salmon stocks prior to their smolting and descending to the sea at the start of their long journey to the rich ocean feeding grounds.

This upper sections ends where the river flows into Loch More. This loch, a literal translation from the Gaelic being the 'big loch', plays an important part in the management of the Thurso for it is the section from the loch, downstream to the sea, that forms the significant part of the fishings.

Perhaps of even greater interest than the river and its fish, its geography and its beats, is the fact that the whole river and even the netting rights all fall under the management of one company, Thurso Fisheries Ltd, under the control of Lord Thurso. For this reason, and because it will probably not be considered unfair to say that management policy, certainly in regard to the role of commercial netting within the overall salmon harvesting scene, could be described as being at variance with current, popular thinking and policy among most rod and line fishermen and interests, the Thurso management calls for some lengthy consideration.

As noted earlier in Chapter 2, Royal Charter granted the salmon fishings on the Thurso to the Earls of Caithness. They were subsequently passed to the Sinclairs of Ulbster during the early part of the eighteenth century.

Salmon were simply not regarded as a sporting asset in those days. Interest in them was confined to the purely commercial. They represented nothing more than a high quality source of protein to be fed to man and beast and which had the added advantage that it could be preserved for winter use by smoking.

The situation of 'all take and no give' was evident in the First Statistical Account of Scotland and Henderson's Agricultural Report published in 1793 which spoke of the earlier productivity of the Thurso but concluded: 'that River has lately been mismanaged by fishing in the close of season, and keeping the cruives shut all the year round. It will require a jubilee to recover its former amount.'

The Thurso at Westerdale showing excellent, streamy water. Some stretches, however, are slow flowing and require 'backing up' to fish the fly successfully

Much the same sorry state of affairs continued into the nineteenth century. It was then, with the growth of the British Empire and the sporting interest and ideals of Victorian society, principally the newly rich upper-middle class, that long-established attitudes to the salmon resource began to change. Those home on leave from soldiering and other colonial appointments sought sport to while away their time. But the remotest parts, and there were not many remoter places than the northernmost tip of Scotland, were really opened up with the coming of the railway.

Towards the end of the century, Sir Tollemache Sinclair, aided by the sporting entrepreneur William Dunbar, was turning his thoughts to developing the Thurso as a sporting rather than simply a commercial asset. The co-operation between Sir Tollemache and Dunbar was described by W. A. Adams in 1889.

> Dunbar leased from the proprietor the whole of the fishings and shootings from the sea to the Sutherland march . . . Acting upon his advice the proprietor opened up the main strath, by making a road from the county road at Strathmore past Dalnawillan and Glutt to join the road at Braemore and on to Dunbeath . . .

At this time, the entire salmon fishing on the Thurso river was let to just six rods. Equally, most of the fishing, besides that on the slow flowing, deep-water sections such as those found in the linns of Strathmore, was undertaken on Loch More. In its time, the loch was described as the best salmon fishing loch in Scotland. Be that as it may, Sir Tollemache Sinclair was obviously concerned that the whole of his asset was far from being exploited to the full, and he looked for further means of improving not only access to the entire river, and improving the accommodation to attract more paying guests, but also of improving the river itself.

He sought advice, mainly from P. D. Malloch, on how to improve the river fishings. The solution suggested was to improve the river at the expense of the fishings on Loch More. A dam, with a fish pass, was built across the outflow, together with smaller dams on some trout lochs in the upper river.

Since that time, when the loch is full of impounded water following a spate, its area is about 550 acres. With an average depth of about 14ft, it holds roughly six weeks' worth of fishing water.

The original intention in designing and constructing the dam was to create a head of water to be used to create artificial spates. However, it was quickly found that an artificial spate, in periods of dry weather, rather than attracting fish into the river, tended to drive them away. The result was that rather than increasing the river catches, artificial spates were forcing fish into the bag nets in coastal waters. Also, the additional dams on the upper water trout lochs were found to be hardly worth the effort of operating them, and so they were quickly abandoned.

Nowadays, the sluices on Loch More are set so as to maintain the river for as long as possible at a height of 10–12in, measured on the marker at Halkirk. In other words, Loch More is used to maintain rather than create a suitable height of fishing water.

The other major development carried out by Sir Tollemache was the building of

Long Pool on the Thurso. The Thurso management were among the first to experiment with maintained summer flow

a hatchery at Braal near Halkirk, with smolt rearing pens set in a nearby burn.

Such was the situation when the present Lord Thurso's father took over the management of the river system in 1912. The Thurso now had the benefit of two very important management tools in the dam and the hatchery. However, catches had not really increased significantly, the only change being that now the salmon were being caught in the river rather than the loch. In fact, the loch was hardly worth fishing, except when prolonged periods of drought reduced it to its former levels. Shallow water is a feature of top-class salmon lochs. So, with no more fishermen visiting the river and the only change being that they now concentrated their efforts on the Thurso, it might have been said in 1912 that, in spite of the heavy investment of time, money and effort, what the Thurso management had gained on the swings, they had lost on the roundabouts.

What else could be done? As many sea netting stations as possible were bought up or leased between Strathy and Dunnet, in order to leave them unfished. The present Lord Thurso states that this was found to be expensive and, in his view, wasteful. Certainly the practice was quickly discontinued.

More effort and money were put into river improvements and to deal with silting problems at Loch More. To give some idea of the scale of this investment, £557 was to be spent in July 1919, compared with an estimated normal annual running cost for the upkeep of the river of £438. Despite these improvements, catches at the time did not improve dramatically, but rather showed a slow, steady improvement. The year 1909 had produced 515 salmon. This was not bettered until 1916 which produced 543. Catches peaked in 1920 with a catch of 1,111 but, such is the way of things when managing a wild resource, slumped to 516 in the following year.

All this time, enormous efforts were made to let the fishings. Thoroughly modern marketing techniques, such as the production of brochures and discounts rising to as much as 25 per cent for any person prepared to take the whole river, were exploited. The river was divided into eleven beats, including Loch Beg, each of which was probably fished by a single guest, aided by a gillie.

It was now, however, that further problems arose for the Thurso management. With the end of the Great War, what was left of the younger generation of Europe were returning to their homes and, the British had been told, to 'a land fit for heroes'. However, the reality, in Thurso as elsewhere throughout the country, was massive unemployment. The 'great' war had ended, but those who had fought through it found themselves heading fast into the 'great' depression.

Leaving politics behind, many of the men of Thurso obviously felt that in a land fit for heroes, the heroes might expect to be allowed to fish for salmon. 'The Comrades of the Great War' under their Commandant Baillie Brims, who was later to become Provost of Thurso, threatened to take over the river for themselves. The situation was resolved at a public meeting in Halkirk at which an angling association was formed under the chairmanship of Mr Black, a teacher, and the Thurso management offered free fishing permits. Besides a system of free salmon fishing for certain local people, stretches of the river were set aside for local trout fishers.

Some sense of normality was resumed, but the management was still faced with the problem that only eight rods were fishing beats 3 to 15. The waters above Westerdale, for instance, were not felt to be sufficient for more than six rods.

It was not until some time in the thirties that the system of rotating two-rod beats was introduced. In the final years of the previous Lord Thurso's management, immediately after World War II, the river was finally reaching something like its full fishing potential. Other than beats 1, 6 and 7 which were left out of the new system, the rest were let as eight two-rod stretches. In the autumn, however, in accordance with past practice, the fishings were attached to the shootings, rather than being let separately.

A magnificent, 20lb spring salmon taken on a fly

(Above) *'Happiness is salmon shaped' – a nice summer salmon*

(Left) *High water on the Hampshire Avon, and thoughts immediately turn to the spinning rod*

It was in 1965 that the present Lord Thurso persuaded his father that the river management should be in the hands of a company. The great fear was that death duties might require the breaking up and selling off of parts of the river, thus putting an end to its unified management. It was for this reason that Thurso Fisheries Ltd was formed and the ownership shared, whilst maintaining the management system.

The early management of the company was greatly aided by the River Superintendent, David Sinclair, who started his career as a gillie on the river. Between them, he and the present Lord Thurso developed the rotation system of beats as it exists today; that is twelve rotating two-rod beats. Set aside from the system is one small beat, known as Lord Thurso's beat, where he can have a cast himself, or entertain friends or special visitors. The other beat outside the rotation system is beat 1 which was extended into a three-rod stretch to be used by the Thurso Angling Club.

Incidentally, the beats are numbered 1–13, excluding the private beat, moving upstream. Thus beats 1–4 lie from Thurso Bay to Halkirk, beats 5–9 from Halkirk to the junction with the Little River, and 10–13, as well as Lord Thurso's beat, between the Little River and Loch More, with beat 12 including Loch Beg.

In order to fish the Thurso, guests must stay at the Ulbster Arms Hotel in Halkirk or at the Lochdhu Hotel. Under the rotation system, two guests are allowed on each beat, and the beats rotate downstream by two each day. As there is no Sunday fishing for salmon in Scotland, this means that, in a six-day week, a pair of fishermen will fish six different beats and experience the full range of the river from Loch More down to the sea; if they stay for a fortnight they may fish beats 12, 10, 8, 6, 4, 2 in the first week and 13, 11, 9, 7, 5, 3 in the following week. Each beat has 8–10 productive pools to occupy the fishing day fully and avoid overcrowding.

A possible bone of contention between those fishing the beats and Thurso Fisheries Ltd is that the estuary nets are kept in operation while, on other rivers, large sums of money have been paid by rod and line interests to buy out netting rights and put an end to their harvest, thus freeing more fish to enter the river. Why is it that Thurso Fisheries Ltd continue to operate these nets?

In an article in *Countrysport* magazine, Lord Thurso explained his thinking on the matter in relation to the general nurturing and intensive stocking programme carried out each year by the hatchery staff.

The estuary net pays for all these improvements and pays the ghillies through the winter when the maintenance and hatchery work is being done. Without the estuary net, fishing and fishing hard from June to 26th August, the management of the river would fall apart. 'But', you may ask, 'if you took off the net would you not catch so many more fish that it would compensate and allow you to put on more rods?' The answer is 'No!'

When conditions are good for fish to run and fish to get caught they will run and they will get caught, net or no net.

(Top) *February snow on Kilphedir Pool, Beat 2 below, on the Helmsdale*

(Bottom) *Early season fishing on a Highland river*

Fishing Beat 12 of the Thurso. Like all rivers in this region, the Thurso is 'fly only'

He cites an example of what can happen when the net is not in operation.

> In 1972 when we had a near record catch in the estuary and, therefore, decided to stop fishing at the end of July, with masses of fish still dancing in the bay, only 403 fish were caught by rods in August, while 2,000 died of suffocation in the 3 lower beats after running in on a 4 inch rise in water.

Well, it is always right to look at each river on its individual merits, and nobody knows his own river better than Lord Thurso. And, of course, this is one of the few rivers where the bulk of revenue generated by netting may be ploughed directly back into the river.

Lord Thurso was also able to discuss his philosophy on how rod and line fishing should be conducted on beats, a system which relies on keeping the rules of the river as simple as possible. Keep the rules simple and clearly stated, and there is little room for argument or misinterpretation. Thurso rules are perhaps as straightforward as they come. There are really only two of them. Only two guests may fish one beat at a time. Fishing is by fly only.

Nothing complicated in that, and yet there have been cases where people, otherwise considered to be highly respectable, have deliberately chosen to break the rules. One party which was caught spinning its beat had to be banned. Another party, found to be fishing three at a time, got a severe and final warning, as did the gillie who had been accompanying them at the time. As Lord Thurso rightly said:

> It is sad, though, that it is necessary not only to watch for poachers but also to watch for anglers cheating on themselves and their fellow sportsmen.

THE HELMSDALE

The proprietors of the Helmsdale, like the management of the Thurso, are fortunate to have the benefit of a significant management tool – a reserve of water to maintain fishing heights in the river. In the case of the Helmsdale, sluices were built to impound water in Loch Badanloch and Achentoul Loch, also known as Loch an Ruathair. This has been significant in making the Helmsdale what it is, and nothing much has changed since W. L. Calderwood wrote at the start of the century, in *The Salmon Rivers and Lochs of Scotland* that 'for ideal conditions of salmon angling with the fly there is no river which surpasses the Helmsdale, and very few which may be compared with it'.

As must be expected on a river worthy of such a description, the fishings on this small but delightful Sutherland river, set in the magnificently wild scenery of the Strath of Kildonan, are not easy to come by. Access to the beats is jealously guarded. Indeed, after April, the proprietors, who manage the entire river in a style of co-operative, virtually keep the river for themselves. Details such as just how many salmon the Helmsdale produces in a season are jealously guarded secrets, but nobody would argue that it will be a four-figure sum. A large proportion of this catch will be taken in the period April to July, which enjoys the peaks of the salmon and grilse runs.

However, you don't have to wait until April to catch salmon on the Helmsdale. The season opens on 11 January, and there is every chance of a fish even at this early date. On the other hand, you have to remember the nature of a Highland winter. It is not uncommon for the river to freeze over in January or February. Many an early season fisherman on the Helmsdale has started his day by helping the gillie to break the ice away from a pool in order to be able to fish. At first thought, it might be imagined that the disturbance of ice breaking would put the salmon off the take. In reality, certainly on plenty of occasions, the reverse is true and the disturbance may actually bring them on to the take, rather than putting them off.

What does put an end to any chance of success with the early season Helmsdale salmon, as it would on any river, is the formation of those accursed ice crystals, in suspension in the water, that are known as grue. With grue in the river, experience has shown that you might as well fish in a bucket for all the salmon you are likely to catch. The only good thing about it is its passing which, again, can be a good time to find a salmon prepared to take an interest in the fisherman's fly. And fly it will be. No other lure is allowed.

To understand how the fishing is conducted on the Helmsdale, it is necessary to be aware of its ownership and how, as already mentioned, the proprietors co-operate with each other. There is a total of six proprietors, with Torrish being the lowest then, moving upstream, Kildonan, Suisgill, Borrobol, Badanloch, and finally Achentoul up at the source of the river. Rather than each proprietor simply having his stretch of the river, they decided to divide the total of what they had into twelve beats, six lying above Kildonan Falls, and six downstream of it.

Incidentally, besides Kildonan Falls being a convenient geographical point to use for dividing the river into upper and lower, it also affects the early season fishings significantly. Salmon in the cold water of the opening months of the season nose their way cautiously into the river. Any obstacle to their passage will halt them. For some reason best known to themselves, in regard to surmounting an obstacle, for salmon the critical temperature is 42 degrees. Until the water temperature has risen above that point, no salmon will surmount the Kildonan Falls. Therefore, until that warmer time, early season salmon fishermen can safely ignore the upper river.

Returning to the twelve beats themselves, those upstream of the Falls are numbered 'one to six above', and those downstream 'one to six below'. Number one below beat therefore lies closest to the sea, running in fact from the Marrel Pool to the head of Salscraggie. Number one above beat, on the other hand, lies immediately above the falls, from Kildonan Bridge to Suisgill Lodge water gauge.

Each proprietor has two beats on any given day, one above and one below the Falls, both of the same number. For example, on a given day, the Torrish proprietor may have number one beat below and, therefore, will also have number one beat above. The beats are then fished in rotation, the next two beats being fished on the following day. Thus each proprietor has access to all of the twelve beats over the six-day course of a fishing week. Beats rotate at 8 pm.

Each proprietor can fish two rods. It is up to them to decide if they will fish together on one beat, or split themselves between the above and below beat. In the early part of the season, before salmon have surmounted the Kildonan Falls, each below beat will be shared between the two fishermen as the above beat will be untenanted by fresh fish.

Later on in the year, particularly during the heavy summer salmon and grilse runs of June and July, many believe that the state of the tide has a heavy influence on whether the above or below beat will offer the best chance. Those lucky enough to fish the Helmsdale at this time of year do not hang about when changing beats. Locals have learnt long ago to watch out for cars with rods strapped to their roofs

Fishing Beat 6 below on the Helmsdale

racing from one beat to another as if they were entered for the Monte Carlo Rally!

At the start of this chapter, it was mentioned that the technique of 'dibbling', like 'backing-up', is very popular on rivers lying north of the Great Glen. Some would say that dibbling has its true home on the Helmsdale. Wherever its birth-place may have been, dibbling is certainly a popular alternative to standard fly fishing techniques on this river.

Basically, dibbling is nothing more than a rather specialised technique for fishing a dropper. As you will know, a dropper is a second fly tied to a short length of nylon attached some 3–4ft above the point fly. Now, that is the normal style of dropper for salmon fishing but, for dibbling, the dropper may be tied much higher up the leader. For many experts using a 10ft leader, the dropper would be attached some 6ft above the point fly, and therefore only 4ft below the tip of the fly line. Another difference is that, while the standard dropper link is only about 3–4in long, the dropper length for dibbling can be about 8in.

Having prepared a suitable leader, the Helmsdale fisherman then has the task of choosing a pair of flies. In order to understand the choice that he makes, we must know something of the technique of dibbling.

The dropper has to be made, quite literally, to dibble across the water surface, just like fishing a bob fly on the surface of a loch. The plan is to stroke the fly across the surface as it swims across, causing it to hover here and falter there, possibly dropping briefly below the surface but for most of the time to be scratching away, cutting a furrow on the surface of the stream. It is a technique involving a short line and preferably a fairly long rod.

If the dropper fly is to behave in this way, it must have a fair measure of presence in the water. Double hooks, a size larger than the point fly, are popular for this technique, and the dressing should be on the heavy rather than the slim side. Favoured patterns, in hairwings, include the Willie Gunn and Stoat's Tail, with a Garry Dog normally being held in reserve for high water. A list of other popular dibbling flies must include the Shrimp Fly as well as the Invicta, Elver Fly and Fiery Brown.

Dibbling is obviously a method to be used on the fast broken headstreams of the river pools. In low-water summer conditions, salmon will congregate in these streams. Such fish, when they have been in the river for some time, are not easy to tempt. The dibbler goes on and on casting and working his fly over the likely area in the hope that one of the fish will be irritated into snatching at the strange object passing over its head. There are times when a salmon will come to a dibbled fly on its first presentation, but it is just as likely to be on the sixth or sixtieth cast.

Hooking a risen salmon, like hooking a big trout that rises to a dry fly, is an art in itself. If only all the salmon would oblige by taking the fly positively and turning back to their lies with it, things would be much easier. The late Jim Pilkington, described as one of the greatest exponents of dibbling on the Helmsdale, said that he hooked about six out of ten offers. Some folk would be happy to do half as well. That said, dibbling has proved itself to be a consistent method of taking salmon when the Helmsdale shrinks under summer skies and, of course, the sense of not knowing quite what will happen next adds to the general air of excitement!

Incidentally, besides his success with the dibbled fly, Jim Pilkington was also the designer of a fly that bears his name. It is a fly that most people associate with cold water conditions at the start of the salmon season, to be tied on tubes, Waddingtons or 'Brora' wire shanks. The Pilkington has a black body ribbed with flat silver tinsel with the all-round wing being three bunches of bucktail: red, blue and yellow, each occupying one third of the shank.

Before leaving the Helmsdale, let us take one last look at its twelve beats in more detail. Looking at the lower beats first, these will see virtually all the fishing activity up to mid-March when temperatures should have risen to the point where salmon will pass the falls. Number one beat below, already described as running from the Marrel to the head of Salscraggie, has five excellent holding pools – upper and lower Caen, the Sand, the Alder and the Stall.

Number two beat below runs from Salscraggie to the tail of the Wood Pool. Pools include the magnificent Kilphedir – 300yd of excellent water which could hold a fisherman's interest for the entire day, were it not for the alternative attractions of the other five pools on this beat including the Upper Torrish. Besides giving its name to that most beautiful of classic, traditional salmon flies, a gem of silver, yellow and black, it was in this pool that John Rutherford of Kildonan House hooked a mighty fish that he played for three hours, during which time it ran three miles upstream. It weighed 45lb, and Mr Rutherford must have been more than pleased with this tremendous achivement on a fly rod.

Number three beat below runs from the Wood Pool to the tail of Baddywood. Number four beat below takes from Baddywood up to Kilearnan Bridge. The sluggish pools on this beat may not look fishable to the uninitiated, but can be productive to the backing-up technique. Chances here are at their best in fairly high water and with an upstream breeze to put a chop on the surface of the flat sections.

Number five beat below runs up to the head of Whinney Pool. Much of this is streamy water. Foam Pool is reckoned by some to be the best spring pool on this beat; it also includes the Duible and Short Pools. This beat, and number one above, are rated as the best for sea trout on the river.

Number six below, the last of the beats below Kildonan Falls, takes us from the head of Whinney Pool to Kildonan Bridge. This stretch contains the great spring pools – Dyke, Church, Manse, Little and Big Rock.

Number one above runs from Kildonan Bridge to Suisgill Lodge water gauge. This, and the next two beats, are very productive as it is into them that the main spawning burns empty themselves. Salmon rest here, having surmounted the falls, until spawning time.

Number two above runs from the water gauge up to the island above Surfaceman's House. Number three above stretches from the island to Kinbrace Railway Bridge, a long stretch containing eleven pools.

Number four above is from the railway bridge up to the junction of the Bannoch Burn. Obviously, this burn is hundreds of miles north of the place of the same name whose very mention stirs the heart of any Scotsman with patriotic blood running in his veins, but this more northerly Bannoch Burn also has its place in history – the history of salmon fishing rather than simply Scotland. As mentioned earlier, folk are secretive about catches made on the Helmsdale, but it has been reported that this one beat had 599 salmon during the season of 1979, with 31 on the best day and 94 for the best week.

Number five beat above is from the junction of the Bannoch Burn up to Loch Achnamoine. This beat, like number four below, needs wind in order to show its best. Finally there is number six beat above, also known as the 'Loch Beat' because it consists of Loch Achnamoine.

It would be hard to highlight just one reason for the Helmsdale being such a fine

The Flats Pool on the Helmsdale

salmon and grilse river. January, February and March all show a steady trickle of the highly prized springers with spring catches rising to a peak in May. Then come the fantastic runs of summer salmon and grilse. Certainly the natural characteristics of the river are highly conducive to salmon, but there is more to it than that. The co-operation of the proprietors must play an important part, leading to a unified code of management.

   As already stated, the sluices on the two upstream lochs are significant management tools in allowing the river flow and run-off to be controlled. If required a short sharp spate can be laid on, but the usual rule, as on the Thurso, is to let a steady stream of the impounded water to maintain the river at a good fishing height. In times of summer drought, when other rivers are crying out for rain, the Helmsdale keeps fishing.

Of course, this serves to increase the numbers of fish caught, but its contribution to enhancing the salmon population may be minimal, unless it is to get them into the river and away from the nets. Far more significant in improving and maintaining a high salmon population, and therefore a significant surplus for harvest, may be the stocking programme. In the autumn, as spawning time comes upon the Helmsdale, some 200 salmon are netted from number three above beat, where they are gathered at the mouths of spawning streams. These fish are stripped of their eggs and milt. The eggs are then transferred to Ardgay for hatching. The fry produced, rather than being returned to the main river or spawning streams to compete with the naturally hatched stock, are released into those streams that are inaccessible to salmon. Salmon may not be able to ascend some streams in order to spawn, but that does not stop salmon smolts descending them at the start of their journey downstream to the sea and off to the food-rich ocean.

In this way, the productivity of the entire Helmsdale system is maximised. Here is a valuable lesson for other rivers. Few things happen by accident and, as many fishery managers will confirm, presuming you start off with the right sort of natural resource, after that it is very much a case of being able to get out no more than you are prepared to put into it.

THE BRORA

The rule on the Brora, as on all the Sutherland rivers, is that fishing will be by fly only. Perhaps this creates a drive in those who live or visit here to bring their fly fishing to perfection and to seek out new techniques and tackle to meet all eventualities. Besides many outstanding patterns of salmon flies designed here, the Brora has also seen the design of what Bill Currie, that great writer on salmon fishing, has chosen to call the 'near perfect salmon fly'.

Basically, these Brora-style, wire-bodied flies are nothing more than a double Waddington shank, except that the shank is made of a heavier gauge of wire so that it fishes less erratically. Onto this shank are tied local favourite patterns such as the Sunrise and Sunset, the Pilkington and the Willie Gunn – local favourites, but the fact is that the Willie Gunn, in a relatively short space of time, has proved itself on rivers far and near. With its gold-ribbed black body and mixed wing of black over orange over yellow bucktail it has, for many fishermen, become practically the only fly that they will tie on when fishing the sinking line at the opening and close of the season.

But what of the river?

The upper Brora is fed by two main tributaries which originate on the Ben Armine Forest and Borrobol Forest. The two tributaries, the Blackwater flowing off Borrobol and the upper Brora off Ben Armine, join at Balnacoil. From here, it is but a short journey of about two miles before the river empties into Loch Brora, a water some four miles long and half a mile wide.

The loch empties into the lower Brora which is a relatively short section only about three miles long. The lower river is divided into two beats, with some twenty main pools, the best of which are probably the Magazine, Pot, Benzie, Madman, Rallan and Ford. These lower river beats are owned by Sutherland Estates on the south bank and Gordonbush Estate on the north bank. In fact, Gordonbush is the principal proprietor on this river system, having rights on both the lower and upper Brora as well as the Blackwater.

Many fishermen are put off by the thought of single-bank fishing. They worry about what the other side might be getting up to, when their backs are turned. However, there is good co-operation between the two estates. They have introduced the system whereby tenants start at opposite ends, working up or downstream as the case may be, so that the changeover is made at 1.30 pm. At no time do any of those fishing the lower Brora have to tolerate an angler on the opposite bank. This lower river is a delightful series of boulder-strewn rapids and long, deep pools. In a hard winter, the lower beats are most likely to produce a springer when the season opens on 1 February, but, if the weather is at all mild, fish may be caught above the loch.

In the opening months of the season, Brora beats can experience very high water levels as a result of heavy rain or snow melt. On most rivers, particularly those with a fly-only rule, this would cause some severe fishing problems but Brora fish, thank goodness, continue to take a cleverly presented fly.

Backing-up is a technique that can work well on the Brora, both at the start and later in the season. Pools particularly suited to this technique are the Benzie, Rallan and Upper Fannich.

Salmon enter the Brora almost throughout the season, from 1 February to 15 October. An average season will produce about 800 salmon. The spring runs gave cause for concern at one time, but have steadily recovered, with February and March fishings now being reliable. By the end of March, as many as 200 salmon may have been caught. As already stated, unless it is a particularly mild winter, most of these fish will have come off the Gordonbush and Sutherland Estates' beats on the lower river.

It is not just adverse temperatures that can hold salmon back from the upper Brora. There is a bar at the top end of Loch Brora, and salmon need a reasonable depth of water in order to cross it, plus a satisfactory temperature.

Early season fish that cross the bar have a tendency to run and populate the upper Brora beats. Certainly by March or April, the main river should be showing fish up to Balnacoil Falls. As water temperatures increase into May, the entire Blackwater should be populated in its turn.

Sport continues throughout the summer and into the autumn. This is an unusual feature of the Brora, compared with other northern rivers. Whatever the reasons may be, the Brora can experience late runs of relatively big salmon, most of which are taken in the lower river. This is why the normal east coast river season, which closes on 30 September, is extended for an extra fortnight into October. This might be a cause for concern to salmon conservationists, except for the fact that there is a rule that no hen fish shall be killed on the upper river after 15 September and the estate reserves the right to stop angling, often as early as 1 September, on the Blackwater. There is no point in killing the goose that lays the golden egg.

Salmon conservation is also to the fore in deciding the opening date of the season. Why does the Brora not open on 11 January like its neighbours? The answer is that, at this date, the lower river may be full of kelts. However hard we try and whatever measures we take, it is a fact that mortality among hooked and played-out kelts already in a weakened condition is high. Extending the closed season by three weeks gives these kelts a little more time to fall back to the sea and, hopefully, return as prime fish another year.

Proprietors on the lower river have already been described. The loch is jointly owned by the two estates, but fished by the local angling association, as well as a number of hotels which have access to it. The season on the loch does not open until 1 May. The upper river Brora is owned by Gordonbush Estate and all of the Blackwater except for the Ben Armine Water, which is owned by Sutherland Estates. The lower river beats will obviously produce most fish at the start of the season but the upper Brora and Blackwater are the scene for most of the action once fish ascend the loch. These are not stale fish that have been hanging about in the lower river and loch. Once the fish start pouring upstream on the tail of a spate, they will carry their sealice above the loch and catches can be staggering, with experienced fishermen taking double figures in a day.

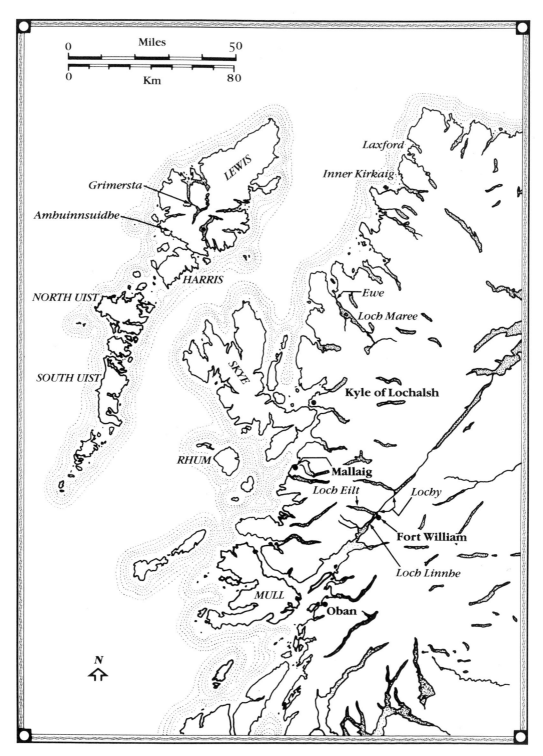

Principal fisheries of the North West Highlands and Western Isles

CHAPTER 8

WEST HIGHLANDS AND ISLANDS

In considering the rivers of Scotland, it is significant that the geographical watershed lies a great deal closer to the west than the east. In consequence, the rivers of the east coast can be characterised as being few in number but large and with extensive tributary systems. The rivers of the west, on the other hand, are far smaller but greater in number. To an east coast fisherman, the rivers of the west might appear as if they have been cut off in their prime and that, if only they had a further thirty or forty miles to run and join up with one another, they could become salmon rivers of real note. If they were to do this, however, they would lose their unique and charming character.

This leads to a problem from the point of view of compiling this description of 'great' salmon beats, namely that, apart from the Lochy, all other West Highland rivers should perhaps be ignored. For example, the Kirkaig river, which is divided into two beats, can produce little more than a hundred salmon in a season. And yet those salmon come off a few miles of what must be almost uniquely beautiful water. Equally, the Awe, which at one time nobody would have hesitated to describe as great, is now but a shadow of itself. Should it be ignored, or will I be excused for including it as an example of what we can lose in the face of man's exploitation or indifference? I hope that I shall be excused, for to ignore the West Highland rivers entirely, purely on the basis that, with one or two exceptions, they are not able individually to produce x number of fish, is to deny the truth in 'there is more to fishing that catching fish', and my own view which says that there must be 'more to the great salmon beats than the fish they produce'. Having said that, a red-letter day on a West Highland river can be an unforgettable experience, with salmon and grilse aplenty for those with the skills to catch them. Of all the salmon rivers in the northern area of the region under consideration, surely the following must be considered the best.

THE LAXFORD

Laxford – the name sounds Scandinavian, and so it is. 'Lax' is Norwegian for salmon and it was in honour of the prolific runs entering this river that early Viking settlers gave it this name.

Its source is at the top of Kinlochbrae from where it flows into Loch More and then through a small lochan before entering Loch Stack. It is below Stack that the true Laxford river begins, flowing quickly to Loch Laxford and the sea. The entire system is the property of Reay Forest Estate, and is very well managed indeed.

A famous river and loch system: surely it must be of some considerable length? The truth is very different and reveals the nature of the West Highland geography. From the top of Loch More to the outflow on Loch Stack is a distance of eight miles. The river itself is little more than three miles. And yet, what sport these few short miles can produce, during the peak of salmon, grilse and sea trout runs in the summer months of June, July and August! Besides the fine variety of fishing on the runs and holding pools of the river, pools such as the Duke's and Duchess's clearly pointing to the Westminster's ownership, there are the two lochs. Loch Stark, in particular, is a great sea trout loch. Indeed, in the forties and fifties, it was widely regarded as the very finest of Scottish sea trout lochs. The sea trout catches of today may not be so prolific as they were then, but that is true of anywhere you may care to mention, and it still ranks as one of the great lochs. Together with Loch More, the two were still producing catches of about 100 salmon and 800 sea trout during the early seventies, when the 3½ miles of river gave combined annual returns of salmon and grilse in the region of 230. Incidentally, a fair proportion of the salmon and grilse would have fallen to the Shrimp Fly which is a great favourite on the Laxford, as on so many of the summer salmon and grilse rivers of the west.

It has been argued elsewhere in this book that netting salmon cannot be justified purely on commercial grounds. I was therefore interested to hear that netting is largely confined to those times on the Laxford when drought and low water lead to heavy concentrations of fish. You will recall, in the description of the Thurso in Chapter 7, an account of concentrated salmon stocks running the river at a time of drought, and vast numbers of them simply suffocating in the reduced flow of the lower pools. A salmon trap, commercially operated in the late fifties and early sixties, is no longer used.

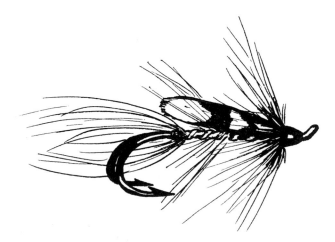

The 'Shrimp Fly' has proved itself to be a deadly pattern for summer salmon and grilse. There are many variations on the theme, and they are all particularly popular on the smaller rivers of the west coast

On the enhancement side of the Laxford's successful equation, a hatchery is sited on the Achfray burn, the normal practice being for some of the ova-hatched fry to be released on the nursery areas and the surplus sold off. The hatchery deals with more than salmon enhancement, and it was from this hatchery on the Laxford that Norwegian sea trout fry were supplied to the Brora and Blackwater.

KIRKAIG AND INVER

I well remember my first visit to these two rivers. It was the Kirkaig, in particular, which caught my attention. It seemed, in many ways, the embodiment of what I had read and heard about the great rivers of Norway, only it was but a fraction of the size, and situated in the north-western Highlands of Scotland. It is a river of steep heather banks and sheer rock faces and cottage-sized boulders. In high water, it is a frothing maelstrom of powerful, churning streams and fast, deep pools. It is a river where waders are out and climbing boots are in, with a number of the fishing stances being no place for the clumsy or faint-hearted.

The Falls of Kirkaig, only two miles above the sea, are insurmountable to salmon. What sport and challenge have been condensed into those two miles!

The Kirkaig is owned by Assynt Estate and is fished by guests staying at the Inver Lodge Hotel, also owned by the estate. In this, as in other examples of salmon beats, it makes a great deal of economic sense for the estate to receive accommodation fees as well as fishing rentals. The river, and its neighbour the Inver, is fly-only, as are all the Sutherland waters. Guests of the hotel, besides enjoying access to the upper, middle and lower beats of the Kirkaig, also gain access to the upper beat of the Inver and, from time to time, the lower beat, the Inver being divided into two.

A factor that may surprise those visiting the Kirkaig beats for the first time is the size of fly used. Although it is mainly summer fishing, the Kirkaig beats fish best after rain to bring the river into spate. Fortunately, the series of lochs above the falls act as a sump where the peat content of the upper water settles and is filtered out, so that the lower river quickly clears, while still running high. In the fast powerful flow, substantial flies are required. A small fly would look totally out of place and quite unnatural stemming that flow. Modern flies such as big tubes and Waddingtons can work well, but many of the Kirkaig's devotees prefer the old-style single salmon iron, in sizes up to 6/0 and with a predominance of classic traditional patterns such as the Black Doctor, Green Highlander, Mar Lodge, Silver Grey, Thunder and Lightning and Yellow Torrish. Also, the dropper can work extremely well. Peter Hay, factor to the Assynt Estate, knows the Kirkaig's fishing as well as any man, and his standard practice, following a summer spate, is to fish a 3/0 on the point and a 1/0 on the dropper.

Purely in terms of fish caught, with perhaps 100 salmon taken off the Kirkaig in a season, the river might not fall into the accepted class of having three great salmon beats. And yet, on its day when the river flows full and clear, thundering down its exceptional glen, and the fisherman uses the traditional flies, casting from some rocky

Loch Assynt, which feeds the River Inver – typical of West Highland loch, short river systems

Gorge-like pool on the Inver

perch set among the high rocks, banks and cliffs, the Kirkaig can provide a great and unique sporting experience.

THE EWE

The Ewe – a short name for a short river. In fact, at little more than a mile long, it has to be one of the shortest rivers in Scotland. Yet, because it is the outflow to the sea from Loch Maree, which is widely recognised as among the finest and most productive salmon and sea trout lochs in mainland Scotland, it can produce plenty of fish and sport. And there are more than a few who say that the loch and its short river are the most ruggedly beautiful in Britain.

It is hard to say exactly where Loch Maree ends and the Ewe begins. Simply by eye, there is a great narrowing of the loch at Coree and Tollie Bay and, with the semblance of a downstream flow, one might be tempted to describe this as the start of the river. However, finer points of geography aside, so far as the fishing is concerned, this is still the loch – a beat to be precise. The demarcation of the top of the river occurs at Top Narrows. From here, through Middle Narrows and on to Lower Narrows there is very little gradient and therefore the water is slow flowing, almost like a series of lochans, and it takes high water to bring on a decent current. An upstream wind is, as on all sluggish river sections, a great aid to fishing. Then the Narrows can show their worth. Top and Middle can produce their salmon, and the Lower Narrows is particularly noted for showing salmon from far back in its tail during conditions of high water.

Below Lower Narrows, the sluggish nature of the river is transformed. From here down, its character becomes one of white water rapids broken by a succession of fine fishing pools, like the Tee Pool, Macordies, Hen, Manse and then the Flats. Here there is a weir with a gap in the middle where running fish halt briefly on their way upstream, and often they can be tempted.

The river divides around a man-made island just below the Flats. The purpose of the island was to form cruives for the netting of salmon. This was a century or more ago when there was little if any demand for salmon fishing with rod and line. Today, all the action is with the fly, and takes place either on the Old Cruive Pool, on the right side, or Hen House Pool on the other. Incidentally, aren't the names of some of our salmon pools incredibly fascinating! You can almost picture the scene as the laird of old and his factor and gillies asked each other, 'Now, what shall we call this one? What about the Hen House Pool? Aye, that's a good one', or words to that effect!

The Ewe is controlled by one estate, and shows its best in July when summer salmon, grilse and sea trout are pouring upstream to the loch. True, as on so many rivers, catches may not be of the same magnitude as those of the past. But there is still a possibility of one rod taking close to double figures of salmon in a day, and the total catch for July is in the three-figure mark.

There is only one more pool to mention on the Ewe. It lies below the great

The River Ewe that flows out of Loch Maree in Wester Ross

thundering stream formed below the island. It is the Sea Pool where the very freshest of fresh fish are taken and, if they are big, sometimes lost. When hooked in the Sea Pool, many a fish takes it into its head to return to whence it came, through heavy white water and on to the sea. Perhaps that is where we will leave the Ewe and its fishermen, on the Sea Pool, reeling in and cursing for the one that got away.

THE LOCHY

To my eyes, and those of many others, the Lochy is the jewel in the crown of West Highland salmon rivers. It is of significant size, taking the flow from the western side of the Great Glen or Caledonian Canal watershed. It is a fine river for fishing, being open and over fine beds of gravel. It is a challenging river to wade and fish, some of the larger pools being better fished by boat. And it is very productive. Just how

A Ewe salmon moves to the fly. Note the 'stooks' in the field – typical of the crofting counties

productive is difficult to say but, as an indication, the relatively short stretch of ticket water available to the public at Fort William can produce 400–500 migratory fish in a season.

Salmon start to run the Lochy in April, these early fish quickly passing upriver. Fishing improves in May, reaching a peak in July and August. In spite of the great volume of water lying above it, the Lochy is best defined as a spate river. Rain falls, the spate comes and, as it falls with the pools coming into ply, the sport with salmon and grilse can be really excellent.

The river, managed by the River Lochy Association, is nine miles long. The fishing, by fly only after the third week in June, takes place on four beats, let by the Association, plus the Mucomir Pool which is a separate let.

Beat 1 is the highest beat, from Croy Pool to Black Cairn Flats, including Pile, Rock, Coulgarmack Pools, Golden Burn and Sandy Haven. Beat 2 is from Bulls Run down to Camisky House. Lochy regulars will recognise names like the Boat Pool, Pothole, Garrowbowie Flats, Loy Mouth, Pollock and Governor Pool. Beat 3 is downstream from Camisky to Torcastle: Fank, Rail End, Rock, Falls, Fence and Garden Pools. Beat 4 is from Torcastle down to Lundy Mouth. Conjure with the names: Cat Pool and the Canal, before trying Lucky Cast, Big Rock Pool, Pol-Na-Ha,

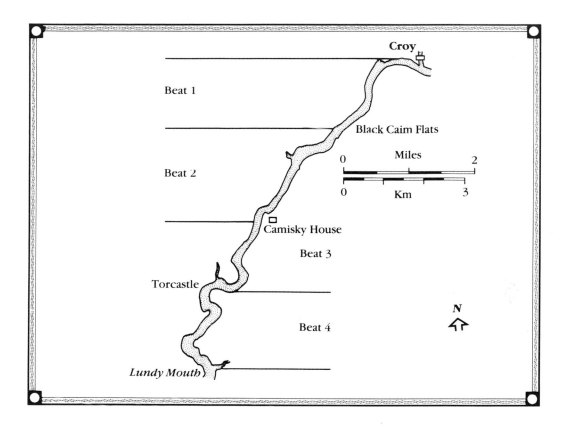

River Lochy beats

Ford Pool, Beech Tree, Rail End and Cruive Pool.

Fry from the hatchery at Camisky are planted out by the River Lochy Association in the main river and its major tributaries. The main tributary is the Spean. It is at the junction of the Lochy and Spean that the Mucomir Pool is found. The Roy joins the Spean about four miles above Spean Bridge. Both these tributaries are salmon fisheries in their own right.

AWE AND ORCHY

If you knew nothing of these Argyllshire rivers, you might think that they were little more than fairly straightforward examples of average quality west coast rivers. But they are far more than that. They are clear examples of how a great river system and its beats can so easily be ruined. So, the Awe, an average river today, but one that we must include in a consideration of great salmon beats because, before it was harnessed for hydro-electricity, was among the very finest of Scottish salmon rivers and with a reputation almost second to none for producing very heavy salmon, the likes of which are seldom seen outside of Norway.

Major A. W. Huntington caught a 57lb salmon on a Mar Lodge 3/0 in July 1921

The Awe and Orchy

from the Cassan Dhu pool. A salmon of the same size had already been taken on fly from the Syndicate Water of the Awe in October 1909, as recorded by Augustus Grimble. Mr H. G. Thornton hooked a salmon in Pol Verie on a 5/0 fly at 1 pm on 12 June 1923; he landed it at 3.30 and it weighed 56lb. The Disputed Pool produced a 53lb salmon in 1913 for gillie A. McColl, who was fishing a Childers fly. Dr C. Child used a Blue Doctor to take his 51lb Awe salmon in September 1907, a fish of the same weight was caught by A. Lees-Milne in October 1913, and Major Huntington, who already had the honour of catching the largest Awe salmon, caught another 51-pounder from the Stepping Stones on a 5/0 Green Highlander in 1930.

These Awe salmon were all taken on the fly, but Mrs Huntington was using bait when she caught a 55-pounder; hooked in Errochd Pool, it was landed in Dalraede. The records do not make it clear whether the following were taken on fly or bait: 54lb, 1877, Sir J. B. Lawes; 54lb, 1880, schoolmaster of Taynuilt.

Such is the list of mighty Awe salmon, and all from a river just three miles long. To include so many salmon of over 50lb in its records is a sure indication of what the numbers of fish of over 40lb must tally, not to mention those of over 30lb. And let us not forget that it is the ambition of many British salmon fisherman to hook, play and land on fly a salmon of over 20lb, which, when the Awe was truly great, must have been a fairly commonplace event. But not today. So what went wrong?

The Awe Barrage was built in the early 1960s across Shallows Pool. There was nothing shallow about the height of the barrage, standing at 59ft high. The entire character of the river was immediately altered, and with the passing of the old Awe went its giant salmon.

Recognition of what the Awe once was should not, however, blind fishermen to the fact that it can still fish well, with a swift flow through the Pass of Brander containing some still excellent holding and fishing pools, on the way to sea-water Loch Etive. It can still produce an occasional fish in the 30lb class. And the Awe fishes earlier, since the erection of the barrage.

To understand this, it has to be realised that Awe fish are running upstream into the 23-mile-long Loch Awe, and on to the Orchy river at its head. Prior to the barrage, fish would pass quickly up the Awe and into the loch. Nowadays, they have the barrage with its Borland fish pass to surmount. In times past, the Awe was not reckoned to start fishing until June. In modern seasons, sport gets under way as early as April, peaking in May–July and carrying through into September.

Incidentally, the Awe season is closed on 30 September. This is entirely by

An historic picture of the Awe, running with a 36-inch spate in the last season before the barrage was built to tame and harness the wild, heavy river

agreement among the proprietors. They could, if they wished, continue until 15 October. The point is that the Awe has no true run of autumn salmon, and they have no wish to catch gravid fish on the point of spawning. Unfortunately, this feeling is not shared by those on the Upper Orchy who continue to fish right up to the legal date.

Fishing on the Awe is in the hands of two syndicates. The river is divided into seven beats from Inverawe upstream to the barrage. In fact, it is more correct to describe the beats as downstream from the barrage to Inverawe. Beat 1 runs from the barrage to the burn at Nether Lorn Hotel, right bank only. Beat 2 is from the barrage to the Oak Pool, left bank; and Shepherd's to Oak Pool, right bank. Beat 3 is from Cassan Dhu to Big Otter, left bank only. Beat 4 is Cassan Dhu to Long Pool, right bank. Beat 5 is Red Brae to Gray on the left bank. Beat 6 is Little Otter to Gray on the right bank. Beat 7, finally, is from Gean Tree to the power station at Inverawe and includes both banks.

Earlier, it was mentioned that a fish was taken by Mrs Huntington on bait. That is no longer allowed. Fishing on all the Awe beats is by fly only.

As already stated, it has to be accepted that the tale of the Awe barrage is not entirely one of loss. The big fish have all but disappeared, but the Awe still enjoys substantial runs and catches. The fish lift in the barrage also allows us to know how many fish run the river. Over the past twenty years, this does, of course, show fluctuations, but the average figure would certainly be in the region of 3,000 salmon and grilse.

Equally, the Hydro-Electric Board have shown that they are prepared to give back to a river from which they take so much. They have provided a salmon hatchery to accommodate 1 million eggs, based near Inverawe House and used by the Awe District Fishery Board to produce fry for planting out in the tributaries of the Awe and Orchy. Adult salmon, for egg and milt stripping, are conveniently taken from the fish lift.

Other than those fish taken by the hatchery staff, the rest of the salmon and grilse will be headed up Loch Awe and into its feeder rivers, the principal of which is the Orchy.

The Orchy is a small but fine river, running out of Loch Tulla through one of the most charming of Scottish glens. Immediately below the loch, there is little fall in the river as it passes through flat heather ground, but then its gradient increases just below Bridge of Orchy and the river is transformed into an ever changing scene of fast streamy runs and holding pools. Further downstream, at the foot of the glen, the Orchy is joined by another main tributary, the Lochy, and from here to the loch the flow gradually falls away, with the river, below the confluence, widening out into a wider and less featured flow.

Black Mount Estate owns the Upper Beat downstream from Loch Tulla. This beat ends at the junction with the Allt Kinglass tributary. The next beat belongs to the Lord Trevor of Auch Estate. Then comes the Inveroran Hotel water, followed by the Craig Estate Fishings. As mentioned when discussing the Awe, the barrage there

The River Orchy at Bridge of Orchy

has a tendency to hold back early-season fish, so these Upper Orchy beats are to be considered as late summer–autumn beats, although, given suitable conditions, salmon can be caught as early as mid-June.

Beats on the Lower Orchy start with a private beat owning both banks down to Catnish, then the Dalmally Hotel fishings on the left bank and the Craig Lodge beat down as far as Dalmally Bridge. Finally there is the Tattersfield Estates beat from the bridge to the junction with the Strae tributary, right bank. Lower Orchy beats normally start fishing in May.

GRIMERSTA

The Lochy at Fort William was described earlier as the jewel in the crown of West Highland salmon rivers. In a similar vein, the Grimersta system has earned itself the reputation of being the most productive salmon fishery in the Hebrides. As little space has been given to the wealth of salmon loch fishing so far in this book, I hope I shall be excused for spending some time considering what many fishermen see as the greatest of great salmon loch systems.

The word 'system' is used because, in reality, the Grimersta fishings comprise a short river, less than 2 miles long, and five lochs. The uppermost loch is Loch Langavat which, at 7 miles long, has the distinction of being the longest loch in the Hebrides. It is followed by Loch Airigh na h-Airde, Loch Faoghail Kirraval, Loch Faoghail Charrasan and Loch Faoghail an Tuim. From this bottom loch the river runs down to the sea lochs, Loch Ceann Hulavig and Loch Roag.

A syndicate system owns the Grimersta, and has done since 1924 when the Grimersta Estate was sold by Lord Leverhulme. At the time of the sale, the property included Garynahine, but this was sold in the seventies, and then again in the eighties. The syndicate has nineteen members, who may invite guests. They stay at Grimersta Lodge and this accommodation, plus the fishery, provides employment for 25 people, a significant number on an island the size of Lewis.

The Grimersta syndicate does not hold exclusive control of all the water in the Grimersta system. Where it does, the rule is that fishing shall be by fly only. One place where it cannot enforce this rule is on the uppermost, 7-mile-long Loch Langavat. This loch is fished by seven estates, and trolling is the most used method here.

Those parts of the system over which the syndicate does have complete control are divided into four beats. Beat 1 includes the perfectly maintained river and the lower half of Loch Faoghail an Tuim. Beat 2 includes the upper half of that loch and the stream connecting it to Loch Faoghail Charrasan. Beat 3 is the stream above Charrasan, Macleay's stream and Loch Faoghail Kirraval. Beat 4, the uppermost beat, is Loch Airigh na h-Airde. At certain times, part of Beat 3 may be included in Beat 4.

Historically, perhaps the Grimersta's most renowned claim to fame is the enormous numbers of fish caught after an artificial spate in 1888. By late August, an exceptionally dry summer had held up great numbers of salmon in the estuary and sea lochs. An artificial spate was created by releasing impounded water on the 22nd of the month. Fish literally ran in their thousands on the stale water from Loch Langabhat. Many people in the fishing world are aware of the incredible catches which followed, but they miss a point that is of great significance for any salmon fishery where this procedure could be carried out. The catches were made in the week following the artificial spate, and after it had started to rain. Up to that time, although it was estimated that perhaps ten thousand salmon and grilse had spread themselves over Beats 1 and 2, only a handful were caught. A sort of piscatorial version of 'you can take a horse to water but you cannot make him drink', suggesting that salmon will run on stale water but require a fresh, oxygenated flow to bring them on the take.

Loch fishing for salmon is generally undertaken with two flies on the leader. The upper fly, fished on a dropper, is often called the 'bob' fly, and that is exactly how it should be worked – with a long, high rod and short line to scuttle it across the wave. Some fishermen like to fish a really big fly on the bob, seeing it as little more than a 'piscatorial dinner gong' to arouse the interest of a salmon, which then falls for the fatal attractions of the smaller and more subtle point fly, swimming close by. This 'little and large' combination is wildly productive on Grimersta. Most regulars will use a big fly on the bob, and by big is meant a size 4 or even a 2. Muddler Minnows with their exaggerated head of clipped deer hair for maximum surface disturbance are very popular. And so is Arthur Ransome's Elver Fly with its vulturine guinea-fowl feathers extending back as much as 2in behind the eye of the hook. The point fly, the one that is actually expected to hook the salmon, will be a small double-hooked fly, size 10 or 12, or a mere wisp of a tube fly armed with the tiniest of outpoint treble hooks.

I had heard that this was the way to fish Grimersta but, as I wrote in another book, although I felt that I must bow to the experience and knowledge of Grimersta aficionados and acknowledging that I had never fished there, I was surprised that far smaller bob flies, as used on practically all mainland salmon lochs, should not be capable of attracting salmon, particularly in the shallow lochs of the Grimersta system. Funnily enough, not long after those words had been published, I was introduced to Sir Gregor MacGregor of MacGregor who is a member of the Grimersta syndicate. He told me that he personally favoured standard-sized bob flies, far smaller than those regularly used on Grimersta, and felt that he certainly caught his fair share of fish. So there we are; a little aside, and a reminder that the words 'always' and 'never' have no significant role to play in any discussion of salmon fishing tackle or tactics.

OTHER RIVERS AND BEATS

This chapter has done little more than touch upon some of the truly excellent fishing available in the West Highlands and Islands. It has, perhaps, given something of the taste of salmon fishing in this area, but I am aware that so much has been left out.

For example, in terms of loch fishing for salmon, close neighbour to Grimersta is Amhuinnsuidhe, which is said to offer some of the finest salmon and sea trout fishing in Europe, with about 250 salmon and 600 sea trout being taken on average in the relatively short summer season. Amhuinnsuidhe is the property of Gerald Panchaud, and is in Harris which, to all practical intents and purposes, is the south end of the same island as Lewis. Anyhow, whatever its geographical position, the quality of fishing available on this estate is clearly indicated by the weekly charge of £9,000 or thereabouts for fifteen folk, with ten fishing, albeit this includes truly luxurious accommodation in Amhuinnsuidhe Castle.

What of the western rivers that have not even been mentioned? Some of the following may never fall into the classification of great rivers containing great beats but, together, they cumulatively come to one of the world's greatest fishing experiences: Hope, Dionard, Kinloch, Polla, Grudie, Daill, Kearvaig and Shinary in the land of the Kyle of Durness and Cape Wrath; Inchard, Duart, Polly, Garvie and Oscaig besides the Laxford, Inver and Kirkaig in north-west Sutherland; the Kanaird, Ullapool, Broom and Dundonnell before the Gruinard and Little Gruinard heading down the coastline towards the rivers of south-west Ross: the Ewe has been mentioned but what of the Kerry, Badachro, Torridon, Applecross, Balgy, Shieldaig, Kishorn and Carron? On into Kintail, Mallaig, Shiel and Morvern districts to find the Ling, Elchaig, Croe, Shiel of Duich, Glenmore, Glenbeg, Arnisdale, Guseran, Inverie, Garnach, Morar, Ailort, Moidart, Shiel, Aline and Rannoch. Then into Lochaber where the Lochy has its companions: Spean, Roy, Arkaig, Loy, Leven and the Nevis that flowed past my office window, on its way off the Ben. Then on across Awe and Orchy to Creran, Etive, Kinglass, Croe, Euchar, Nell and Oude before passing on to Kintyre with its Add, Barr, Lussa, Machrihanish, Breackerie and Conie Waters, the Carradale and Claonaig. And was it right to leave out the Fyne, owned by the Cairndow and Ardkinglas Estates, where so much improvement work is in hand? But could I then have skirted over the Kinglas, Aray, Shira and Douglas before approaching the lowlands past the Ruel, Eachaig, Loch Lomond, Falloch, Leven and Endrick? Now their names have been written and casts remembered where bright silvery salmon run from sea pool to the falls, and rivers and fishermen can join in saying 'What care we for the man who knows only the Spey!'

Explaining the sluices on Loch Eilt where it flows into the River Ailort. There are a host of such small salmon rivers in the West Highlands and islands

CHAPTER 9

CONON AND BEAULY

The Conon and its fairly close neighbour the Beauly are both outstanding examples of medium-sized east coast rivers capable of providing excellent sport. Larger than rivers like the Thurso, Brora and Helmsdale, they are, nevertheless, more intimate than big flows such as the Ness, Spey and Tay and, in the opinion of many salmon fishermen, offer near ideal conditions for fishing the fly.

Of the two, perhaps the Conon is, if not purely from the fishing point of view, the more interesting. In recent times, it has experienced the full range of modern market forces, some good and some, perhaps, not so good. It has been 'hydro-ised' and part of it has been 'time-shared' and still it soldiers on. In many ways, it is a prime example of a river surviving and succeeding in the modern world.

CONON AND BLACKWATER

Largest of the Ross-shire rivers, the Conon is fed by four principal tributaries, the

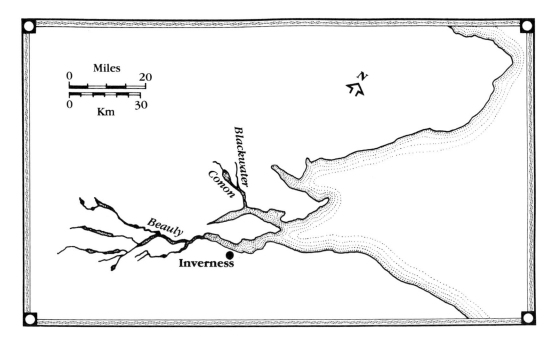

Rivers Beauly, Conon and Blackwater

Blackwater, Bran, Meigg and Orin. The very names have a hint of Celtic mythology about them. Surely, if an ancient hero were searching for names for his three most trusted deerhounds, he could do worse than choose Bran, Meigg and Orin. And they would find a fine, wild home in the high heather moorlands that give birth to the Conon. The tributaries run over peat ground, gradually growing and changing to swift flowing rivers in their own right. Then the arable lands of the lower Conon are reached. Steep-sided glens make way to a soft, arable vale where the Conon takes its time, as if reluctant to join the sea waters of the Cromarty Firth near Dingwall.

A natural scene, or is it? Nine dams – that is the number of obstructions built by the North of Scotland Hydro-electric Board on the Conon and its tributaries. You could say that they have gone dam-crazy in their bid to exploit the energy-giving potential of the system: dams and pipelines, aqueducts and six power stations. The Blackwater and lower Orin, certainly, are no longer able to provide more than a hint of their former glories, except immediately on the heels of heavy rain. And the fishing on the Conon, although in fact today it receives more water than in previous times due to diversion from the upper reservoirs created by the damming, is not what it once was. As has been discovered on other rivers and beats, unpredictable rises in water level due solely to the needs of power generation are not the same thing as natural spates of fresh rain water.

How good was the Conon in former days? Well, I remember hearing somewhere that if you were to drink the Conon water, it would taste of salmon! Perhaps that is true. At times even I, a smoker for many years, can smell the salmon lying in a river. So when there were enough fish, the water would indeed smell of salmon, and taste of them as well.

But the very nature of salmon returning to the Conon has changed, and the changes on Conon may be a pointer to changes experienced on other rivers, whether hydro-ised or not. It is generally accepted that those salmon which run at the start of the season, springers as we call them, make their way gradually up into the furthest reaches of the spawning areas. This had been known for a long time but, until the coming of hydro schemes, it was not realised that, by denying the spring fish access to the uppermost tributaries, they would revert to summer running as salmon and grilse. On the Conon, which had an enviable reputation for producing spring fish, hydro-isation led to the fading away of spring runs, to be replaced by summer fish. At the present time, the Conon can show only a handful of fish from February to April whereas, prior to the hydro in the early sixties, these months might well have produced 200 or more.

Nowadays, May is better than the first three months of the season but the heavy runs of summer salmon and grilse cannot be expected until June, with numbers increasing in July. By early August the runs are fading and, by the middle of the month, few fresh fish are to be found. By the end of the season on 30 September, only stale fish are being caught.

Besides its effect in purely fishing terms, this concentrated bonanza of summer sport, by effectively limiting the season, has radical social and economic consequences which the decision-makers do not seem to take into account. We are all aware of the need to harness energy, but what is the effect on the local community? Summer fish attract visitors at a time when the Highlands are already full of tourists. Spring salmon, on the other hand, extend the tourist season and fill hotels out of their main season. Any rural community must benefit from an attraction that can generate income over an extended period. The extension of this income is denied, except in terms of fishing rents and rates, by concentrating activities into a few months.

Another aspect of modern social and economic forces on the Conon is the fact that, until a few years ago, practically the entire river was owned by the Hydro Board. Then, for fairly obvious reasons and in the modern way of things, they decided that a realisation of the river's capital value would be of greater benefit than a regular annual income. The decisions were made, and the most productive sections, the Brahan Beats, were sold off. Fortunately, other stretches were retained by the Hydro Board to ensure access for locals and visitors who choose to fish on a daily or weekly basis, and who simply could not afford to take a look-in at what happened next. Make a river available, and it seems inevitable that it will be promptly sold off in time-shares. It seemed that all but the Blackwater and Upper Conon would be sold again on a time-share basis.

The estuary below Cononbridge, however, was bought by the Ross and Cromarty District Council to be managed and fished by the Dingwall and District Angling Club for the benefit of locals and visitors alike. Besides obviously making a lot of people happy, this was undoubtedly a wise political move. Heaven knows, there are enough problems in maintaining salmon stocks in the present era, and I am well aware from my own experience in south-west Scotland that the purchase and subsequent sale of a beat on a time-share basis, which had previously been let on a day and weekly ticket basis, does little to gain local or popular support, whatever it may do for the entrepreneur's bank balance. Suffice it to say that we should, at least from time to time, consider our public image.

In contrast, what does do our image on great salmon beats no end of good is the sort of effort made by the Loch Achonachie Angling Club. They were acting, fairly comfortably one would imagine, as managers for the Hydro Board's fishing on both the Upper Conon and Upper Blackwater beats. It was then that the Hydro Board dropped an ultimatum onto their laps: either they would raise the cash to buy the beats, or else the board would put them on the open market, to be sold to the highest bidder and, no doubt, to go down the time-share route. It must have taken an enormous financial effort but, within six months, the Angling Club were the proud proprietors of the Upper Blackwater. It took another 18 months to raise a further £70,000 to purchase the Upper Conon. They were aided in this by the Highlands Development Board and the District Council but, best of all, not only by local anglers but by individuals from all over the country and even as far away, it is said, as Belgium

A salmon on Beat 1 of the River Fyne, Argyll

(Above) *A perfect Dee Springer of 9lb from the Dee*

(Top right) *Fishing the famous Lummels Pool at Aboyne*

(Bottom right) *The author playing a lively salmon in the suspension pool, Mar Estate, upper Dee*

and Iceland. This is a great success story and the effort that went into securing the beats for the use and enjoyment of anglers, half local and half visitors, and for the benefit of the local economy, must surely put them close to the top of a table of social importance in regard to salmon beats.

Salmon do not normally arrive in the Upper Conon via the fish lift and Torr Achilty dam until the early days of June. July will produce more fish, with August and September being better still although the fish are staler at the end of the season. Parts of the river system are fly-only, but spinning is allowed here, with an artificial lure, when the water level is high. The fly, however, provides the mainstay of sport. Regulars will tell you that you need seldom go bigger than a 6, even in high water, and sizes will reduce down as far as a 12 when the levels shrink. Popular patterns include the Stoat, Tosh, Garry, Munro Killer and Hairy Mary. These are, in fact, the most popular summer salmon and grilse patterns on a whole host of rivers.

The other part of the club's water is above the Falls of Rogie on the Upper Blackwater. As on the Conon, fish ascend to the club's water via a fish pass at the falls, the harbingers of the main July to September fish arriving from the early weeks of June. The season of 1987 produced a return of 84 salmon, the bulk of this catch coming in August and September. Again, spinning is allowed in high water. Low water, however, is the general rule because the headwaters are dammed and transferred by aqueduct to the Conon. A spot of local rain is what is required to bring the Upper Blackwater pools into ply, and then the summer sport can be fast, furious and quite outstanding.

Moving downstream, the beat below the Falls is known as the Rogie or Middle Beat. This was bought by a person whose primary intention was not financial, in that his first act upon acquisition was not to sell it off on a time-share basis! He fishes it himself at times in the summer months but, when he does not require it for himself, the beat is let to the public. The effect of the Falls is clearly demonstrated with no fish ascending them until early June, but here, just below the Falls, salmon can be taken as early as late March, but do not expect too many before May. After that, during a summer spate, grilse will literally be pouring into the Rogie Beat, and double-figure catches in a day are not uncommon from the small but rock-girt and boulder-strewn pools like the Flat, Rogie, Sulkie, Square, Step and Turn. And it should be noted that grilse do not need the same heights of water in order to run and take as salmon. Sport with these game little fish will continue into periods of low water.

Below the Rogie Beat is the Bottom Beat and, again, this is owned by an individual who is happy to provide the public with an opportunity to fish on a daily or weekly basis. Also, as on Rogie, this is an owner who is prepared to improve the facilities on his beat. Both the beats that are let on a daily or weekly basis have had new fishing huts erected, and there has been considerable brush and tree clearing to improve access to the fishing stretches. Not only are there similarities in improvement

Summer sport in the Highlands – an 8½lb salmon on a Hairy Mary below Oykel Bridge

works on both the middle and lower beats but, also, they enjoy roughly similar timing of runs. Both can produce early season fish, but sport does not really get into top gear until the arrival of the grilse runs from early June onwards. Incidentally, the rule on the bottom beat is fly-only.

Lest I be accused of ignoring the time-share beats, I must report something about the Upper, Middle and Lower Brahan beats. At the end of the day these were the only Conon beats to be time-shared. For those fortunate enough to have the necessary thousands when these three beats were marketed, they provide excellent sport. Grilse fishing in the summer months can be spectacular, with beats showing their potential to produce 40 fish in a week. In the 1987 season, Middle Brahan was outstanding with 357; Upper Brahan had 145 and Lower Brahan saw 134 grassed. These figures are good, but should be put into context. Before the hydro-isation of the Conon, Lower Brahan used to be able to produce an average of 300 salmon, and that just over the early months of the season. Today, it can struggle to produce double figures from the start of the season on 26 January until the start of May, and the bulk of Lower Brahan sport comes in July, August and September. As might be expected, the upper beat is just that little bit later. As Bill 'Rogie' Brown wrote in *The Haig Guide to Salmon Fishing in Scotland*: 'Upper Brahan Beat . . . is not an outstanding one but can be quite reasonable in August and September'.

THE BEAULY

The Beauly is an interesting river system for many reasons. Firstly, it is one of the few rivers that does not bear the same name throughout its length. This can lead to some confusion. Virtually the top of the system is Loch Affric which flows into Loch Benevean, the outflow of which is known as the Affric river. Then the Affric, just below its junction with the Tomich Burn just upstream of the Fasnakyle Power Station, becomes the Glass. The Cannich river joins the Glass and then, further downstream, when the ever increasing flow has been joined by the Farrar, the river, at last, is known from that point on as the Beauly until it finally empties into the salt water of the Beauly Firth.

This river system, like the Conon, has been harnessed for the production of hydro-electricity. In this case, at least, there are immediate advantages for the local people. Strathglass was notorious for its totally devastating floods. The very real risk to life and land has been removed by the controlling effect of the Hydro Board.

The tributaries are important not only for providing spawning and nursery areas but also as fishing streams in their own right. Indeed, the salmon fishing on the Glass can be very good at times. Lovat Estates own most of the Glass; they have seven beats and Struy Estate has one. Glass salmon run from late July but the river is most productive in August, September and on to the season's close in mid-October, although, by then, fish will have donned their spawning suits.

The Farrar has been hydro-harnessed but is still a valuable spawning area. Lovat Estates tend to use the upper reaches in their ownership as nursery ground, stocking

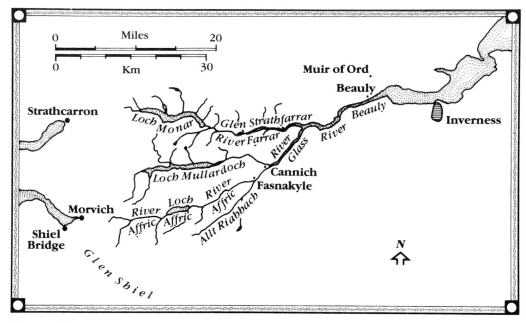

The Beauly system – stretching virtually from east coast to west

with hatchery-reared fry and smolts. The lower Farrar, on the other hand, owned both by Struy Estate and Culligran Estate, is actively fished and can show fair numbers of salmon and grilse.

Moving downstream to the Beauly itself, two dams were built at Aigas and Kilmorack as part of the overall hydro scheme. The effect of these dams has been to flood certain good fishing pools behind them, such as the Red Rock, Mare's and Stone, but little spawning area was lost on what had been a relatively rocky and fast-flowing turbulent section of the river, both the dams being set in gorges.

It is interesting, however, that while fish seem happy to use the Borland fish pass on the Kilmorack Dam, the first one that they meet on their upstream journey, they are not so happy to ascend the Aigas pass. Even with artificial spates to encourage them, it is noticeable that a significant number of fish that have passed at Kilmorack remain below Aigas. For example, in 1965 there were 8,900 salmon and grilse counted at Kilmorack, but only 8,641 at Aigas. In 1971 the figures were 10,621 and 8,954; the following year the discrepancy was far less with 5,356 and 5,315, although on figures of much the same magnitude in 1977, with 5,653 having passed Kilmorack, only 4,912 ascended Aigas.

Whatever fish pass Kilmorack and Aigas, there is no doubting the outstanding quality of the salmon and grilse fishing from Kilmorack down to salt water. The stretch is divided into three beats, all owned by Lovat Estates. The Beauly is a fine, big river flowing through rich agricultural land and hardwoods. Big it may be, but the pools are well suited for the wading fisherman, with pleasant gravel beds. There are, however, a number of deeper, wider pools that fish best with the fly from a boat.

The three beats are known as the Falls, Home and Dounie or Downie. Each is made available to four rods, and this leaves plenty of elbow room. The Falls has eight named pools, the Home has 13 and the Dounie 10. Perhaps the most famous of these pools are the Willow, Fly, Minister's and the far-stretching Long Reach on the Dounie, the Silver and Groams on the Home, and the Ferry and Cruives on the Falls beat. Incidentally, the Cruives is another of those pools which salmon will not ascend until the water temperature is above 42 degrees.

Other beats on the Beauly include the Aigas and Eskadale beats which lie above the Aigas Dam and below the confluence with the Farrar. Once the fish are over the fish passes on the dams, these beats can provide good sport. A total of seven other beats are let on a day-ticket basis, including the estuary beats which are the only ones where spinning is allowed.

The Beauly is not only a delightful river to fish but also a fine example of good management and public access. Lovat Estates undertake the control of the river in regard to upkeep and improvement, and it is said that four-figure numbers of fishermen are able to enjoy the fishing on offer each season. One beat has produced 48 fish in a day and it is not uncommon for one rod to grass a dozen fish. Much of the success of the Beauly beats must be put down to two factors. Firstly, there are two hatcheries producing more than a million fry for planting out. Secondly, the netting rights in the Beauly Firth were bought by the then Lord Lovat during the nineteenth century. Improve the productivity and control alternative forms of harvest: a simple formula but one which Beauly management has shown to be the basis of salmon enhancement.

CHAPTER 10

THE SPEY

The catchment area of the Spey is the second largest in Scotland. Only the Tay is greater. Badenoch, Cairngorm, Grampian and Monadhliath, all these mountain ranges combine to provide a reservoir of snow to melt and fill the Spey with water through the warming spring and on into summer. This maintains the flow at a good medium fishing height, except when hard frosty spells serve notice on the snow melt to cease. If there is to be a drought, it will only happen in the period of July to September, when the snows of all but the very highest and shaded corries are just a memory.

Anybody who understands salmon and salmon fishing will recognise the fundamental importance of the effect of snow melt on the early Spey fishing. High, cool but clear water encourages fish to enter and run the river. There are neither natural nor man-made obstructions to their upstream odyssey. The Spey can be full of fresh salmon and grilse making their steady progress from one holding pool, a particular resting lie, to the next. Fresh fish in clear water are alert, and best prepared to show an interest in the fisherman's offering. Little wonder that so many British and foreign sportsmen place the Spey and its salmon fishing on a pedestal. Add to that the fact that it has emerged as perhaps the greatest of Scottish sea trout rivers, and it is clear why the Spey, to so many, is the game fisherman's dream come true. Mark you, however, the Spey and its fishing is no push-over. For the fly fisherman – and many would contend that a man who would spin or worm the Spey after the start of May would probably steal from his mother – the Spey offers one of the greatest challenges to display his casting abilities, control of the line, and competence in deep wading without drowning. The natural force of the middle and lower Spey as you dare to wade its streams and runs has to be experienced to be believed. Chest waders, long rods and the now famous Spey casting, this is the tackle and technique for facing the Spey. The man who is afraid to wet his thighs and who thinks a rod of less than 15ft is ideal will not make much of an impression, except perhaps when the river shrinks away in summer.

This tackle and technique extends to all the classic, British salmon rivers – certainly the Spey, Tay and Tweed, if not to such a great extent the Aberdeenshire Dee. Those who fish these waters soon learn the need to have thoroughly mastered the crafts of the sport. On wide and long holding pools they recognise the great value of a gillie, unless the fisherman is thoroughly experienced and knowledgeable as to the salmon's lies, where they may rest briefly when running, and their roving routes. They cast as long and straight a line as they can handle, and settle it down like a feather for

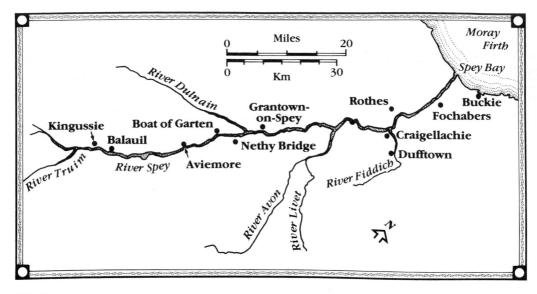

The Spey

minimum disturbance, taking at least one big pace and maybe three or four between casts, and they know to take their time to play a fish when hooked, keeping the rod point well up from a position just downstream of the fish to tire it quickly whilst avoiding the line being drowned.

All these things are important and true on any of the big classic rivers. They are never more true, however, than when the Spey is fished or discussed.

In order to paint a picture of the Spey, it must first be clearly described as being almost two rivers in one. See the Spey in its upper stretches, and you would not recognise it for the great, boulder-rolling torrent that it becomes at about Grantown. You could say that the Spey flows back to front – sluggish and meandering in its upper reaches, but fast and furious in its middle and lower beats.

The accepted source of the Spey is on the slopes of the Corrieyairack Forest on the southern slopes of the Monadhliaths. From here, it is a short journey to Little Loch Spey. From this loch, the Spey flows on sluggishly, in places hardly appearing to move, down past Spey Dam and on through pike-infested waters as far as Newtonmore, where it is joined by the Truim tributary, and then, at Newtonmore itself, by the Calder. On it meanders, through the flooded lands of Loch Insh after having been joined by the Tromie.

Below Loch Insh, the river no longer has the character of an unconscious giant, but it still does little more than stretch a leg and wink an eye at what it is to become when it wakes. The Feshie, having joined just below Loch Insh, dawdles along making no substantial change. But then comes the Druie, just upstream of Aviemore, and this torrential little river charging off the 4,000ft plus northern slopes of Cairn Gorm gives the giant a bit of a shake, but not so much as to make him sit up and take any real notice, and he dozes off into Loch Morlich. After that, from Aviemore

Deep wading as the gillie takes a well-earned rest in the boat on Pollowick Pool

down nearly as far as Grantown, despite being joined by the Nethy and Dulnain, the slumbers continue. Incidentally, the Dulnain, like the Avon that flows into the Spey just below Grantown, is a very important spawning and nursery resource, as well as both of them being grand little salmon rivers in their own right.

And then the Spey, from Grantown downstream to the sea, is transformed. The giant is awake! It flows through a succession of outstanding pools and runs the likes of which can only be matched for the briefest portions of other British rivers and, on some of them, not at all. And what of the great salmon beats of the Spey, and which is the greatest of them all? The choice would be made from the most famous of them, a list that would include if travelling upstream from the sea to Grantown the famed names of Gordon Castle, Orton, Delfur, Aikenway, Rothes, Arndilly, Easter Elchies, Aberlour, Wester Elchies, Carron, Laggan, Knockando, Pitchroy, Ballindalloch, Tulchan and Castle Grant. How could you judge them, one against the other? It would take a braver man than I.

In view of beats changing hands and then being the subject of re-sale on a time-share basis on a growing number of rivers, it is perhaps interesting to note that, of the great Spey beats, very few have changed hands in the last thirty years. This is not surprising. If I had a Spey beat, it would take heaven or hell to get me to part with it!

Before looking closer at these beats and their fishing, the actual salmon themselves have to be considered. Most authorities agree that while it is difficult to judge the remaining quality of the early spring runs, there has definitely been a swing towards ever increasing numbers of summer salmon and grilse. Following the widely publicised restrictions on netting, this phenomenon is likely to continue. If this happens, and there is every reason to believe that it is doing so already, that is all very well for the mid-season fish and fishermen, but it is a far from bright picture for the opening months of the season. It is said that the average weight of Spey salmon is 10–12lb, but this will obviously be affected now that there are such enormous runs of grilse from July through to September.

Spey is not alone in this. The Tay is another classic river which seems to have lost any sort of worthwhile run of early season fish. The reasons are varied, probably being a combination of factors involving high seas fisheries and legal and illegal drift netting, not to mention freshwater poaching on a truly horrendous scale. It would be arrogant to ignore the possible effects of rod and line fishing. Spring salmon are in the river a long time before spawning and, whether it be from the poacher's nets and poisons, the angler's fly, spinners and bait, or natural predators, it is a long time to be at risk. Spring salmon seem to be the most vulnerable of the salmon species. But all this talk of early season tales of woe should not put a smoke screen over the fact that, for richer or poorer, in sickness and in health, the Spey remains the greatest love of many a fisherman, and the most magnificent of salmon rivers.

The best of the Spey fishing, from about Grantown down to Spey Mouth, covers a distance of nearly 50 miles. In this length, it falls about 600ft. In other words, from

The Spey has a host of magnificent pools for fly fishing – Delagyle beat

Grantown to the sea, it descends at a rate of 12ft in a mile, on average. In this section, Strathspey is deep and steep. High banks are common, and it is clear why fishermen on these beats sought to develop a style of casting where line and fly need never travel behind – the style of cast that has developed into the single and double Speys as we know them today.

A distance of 50 miles, on a river the size of the Spey, obviously takes in a considerable amount of water. It also covers a lot of great beats, some of which have already been named. For the purposes of description, a clear distinction can be made. The upper river, above Grantown, can virtually be ignored. Middle Spey will be taken as from Grantown downstream to Rothes, and Lower Spey, obviously enough, from Rothes to Spey Bay and the sea.

MIDDLE SPEY

It is a great advantage on the beats of Middle Spey that they have both banks, the exceptions being Wester Elchies, Kinermony, Easter Elchies and a part of Arndilly which are single-bank fishing. On the other beats, the fishing rights from both banks are owned. These beats are Castle Grant, Tulchan, Ballindalloch, Pitchroy, Knockando, Carron and Laggan and, of course, that part of Arndilly which is not single bank. It gives a far greater sense of freedom and choice, to avoid having neighbours across the way.

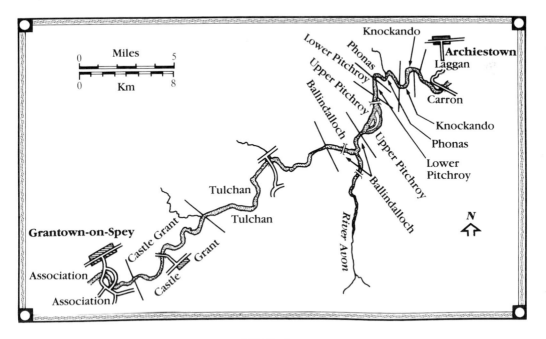

Middle Spey

The Spey near Tulchan

I said earlier in this chapter that it would take a braver man than I to pick out one Spey beat as being greater than all the rest. And, it has to be said, picking a Middle Spey beat is just as difficult. For Middle Spey is widely regarded as the very best of the river – what Miss Jean Brodie might have described as the 'crème de la crème' – and therefore choosing the best Middle Spey and best Spey beat are one and the same thing. Fortunately, I have no need to make that choice. It has already been made by John Ashley Cooper in his book *The Great Salmon Rivers of Scotland*.

If pressed, one might cite Ballindalloch or Wester Elchies as second to none.

It is hard to say now exactly how Ashley Cooper considered the extent of Ballindalloch, and it causes some amusement to see contradictory maps of Spey beats in various publications. Ashley Cooper certainly refers to Pitchroy as a subsidiary of Ballindalloch. However that may be, what undoubtedly goes a great way towards making Ballindalloch such a great beat is that it is here, at the far-famed Junction Pool, that the Spey is joined by the Avon. This is a fine river in its own right, and the Junction sees a great exchange of water from the Avon to the Spey, and the return from the Spey of salmon, grilse and sea trout homeward-bound to the Avon.

The Avon runs for forty miles from just behind Tomintoul, the highest village in Scotland at 1200ft. Incidentally, in pronouncing the name of the Avon, the v and the o are silent, the local tongue saying A'n. Its source, in fact, is recognised as being Loch Avon which lies below the slopes of Beinn Mheadhoin in the Cairngorms. Avon fish will tarry, waiting for a spate to run their parent river, in the pools below and including the Junction.

Outstanding as Ashley Cooper obviously considered Ballindalloch, it seems that he would have given the highest honours to Wester Elchies were it not for the fact that it was single-bank fishing only. As he put it when describing this beat, just above the village of Aberlour:

Such pools as Dailuaine, Pol ma Cree, Delagyle and the Rhynd make an unforgettable impression and can nowhere be surpassed.

Ashley Cooper also made mention of George McCorquodale of Dalchroy, who fished the Spey from 1891 to 1935. Those readers who have already turned the pages of Chapter 1 will recognise G. F. McCorquodale as employer of Dugald Macintyre, the keeper, sportsman and writer. Macintyre described his employer as about the best of the very many good salmon anglers that he had watched. Ashley Cooper goes a stage further, and this is more than interesting from the man who, deservedly, is described by many as the greatest salmon fisherman, certainly of modern times. Ashley Cooper wrote of McCorquodale that he was probably the greatest salmon fisherman of *all* time. He killed 8,924 Spey salmon, mainly on Tulchan, but also on

The junction of Avon and Spey near Ballindalloch

Playing an April Spey salmon on Pol Ma Chridh on the Delagyle beat near Aberlour

what is now the Brae Water at Gordon Castle which he fished in spring and autumn.

Where the two writers differ, however, is in their accounts of McCorquodale's techniques. Ashley Cooper describes him as a 'fly-only man' but Macintyre who, after all, should have known his master's fishing tastes as well as any man stated:

Mr McCorquodale personally informed me that he believed a fly was actually the best lure for salmon, when the state of the river was such as to justify its use. His idea, however, was to catch salmon when he went fishing for them, and to compass his ends he used all legal lures for the fish.

As if to emphasise this point, Macintyre then went on to describe some Devon minnows that McCorquodale had made up for his use. He was obviously a wealthy man. The Devons were made from sterling silver for a softer gleam to attract the fish. Spinning in those days was a far cry from the relative ease of modern casting reels and lines. The minnow was lobbed out underhand, with the line being coiled in the left hand as it was recovered.

Before leaving Middle Spey, it has to be said that, while it has already been mentioned that the average size of Spey salmon is in the region of 10lb, very much larger fish are fought and beaten or lost each season. Indeed, together with the Wye and Tay, the Spey is one of the best prospects for coming to grips with a truly big salmon in British waters. The largest Spey salmon taken on rod and line was in fact grassed on the lower river – in the Dallachy Pool of the Gordon Castle Water. It was taken on a size 4 Carron fly by Mr W. G. Craven in the autumn of 1897 and, surprisingly, took only a quarter of an hour to play out. But the most celebrated of Spey salmon was, undoubtedly, that caught by Duncan Grant, a shoemaker in Aberlour, who, in the custom of the time before salmon fishing became so commercially attractive and protected, decided one day to take an hour or two's fishing in some of the pools above Elchies Water. What happened next was to be fully described by William Scrope in *Days and Nights of Salmon Fishing*. The year was 1810, and the month was July:

Duncan tried one or two pools without success, till he arrived at a very deep and rapid stream, facetiously termed 'the Mountebank'. Here he paused as if meditating whether he should throw the line or not. 'She is very big', said he to himself, 'but I'll try her; if I grip him he would be worth the hauding.' He then fished it, a step and a throw, about half way down, when a heavy splash proclaimed he had raised him, though he missed the fly. Going back a few paces, he came over him again and hooked him. The first tug verified to Duncan his prognostication, that if he was there 'he would be worth the hauding'; but his tackle had thirty plies of hair next to the fly, and he held fast, nothing daunted. Give and take went on with dubious advantage, the fish occasionally sulking. The thing at length became serious; and after a succession of the same tactics, Duncan found himself at the Boat of Aberlour, seven hours after he had hooked the fish, the said fish fast under a stone and himself completely tired. He had some thoughts of breaking his tackle and giving the thing up; but he finally hit upon an expedient to rest himself, and at the same time to guard against the surprise and consequence of a sudden move by the fish.

He laid himself comfortably on the banks, the butt end of his rod in front; and most ingeniously drew out part of his line, which he held in his teeth. 'If he tugs when I'm sleeping', said he, 'I think I'll find him noo'; and no doubt it is probable that he would. Accordingly, after a comfortable nap of three or four hours, Duncan was awoke by a most unceremonious tug at his jaws. In a moment he was on his feet, his rod well up and the fish swattering down the stream. He followed as best he could, and was beginning to think of the rock at Craigellachie, when he found to his great relief that he could 'get a pull on him'. He had now comparatively easy work; and exactly twelve hours after hooking him, he cleicked him at the head of Lord Fife's water; he weighed fifty-four pounds, Dutch, and had the tide lice upon him.

LOWER SPEY

As you would expect, the Lower Spey is noticeably larger than the middle and upper parts. Its size is swelled by a number of streams and burns, the principal one of which is the Fiddich, whose glen lends its name to but one of the famous Speyside malt whiskies.

Also, because the river is now flowing through a softer and more arable area, it has a tendency to spread outward, pushing back the less stable banks. Thus men have to lend a hand, and soft shingle banks are reinforced to withstand the erosion of spates, and groynes are built to aid the main current and maintain shingle in place, which might otherwise fill the salmon's rocky lies. Adding to this problem of riverside maintenance on Lower Spey beats is the fact that, whereas on upstream beats it is common to have riverside trees, here they are far more widespread. If there were more trees, of course, their roots would serve to strengthen the soft banks.

However that may be, the pools of the Lower Spey are very wide, necessitating long casting. Equally, they are very long. For example, on Orton beat, Cairnty is at least 600yd long, and there are similar pools at Delfur. Obviously, the fisherman must get a move on, and there is little point in shuffling along at one pace between casts. Such pools do, in fact, show us all just how little is the amount of water that we may limit ourselves to covering in a day. If, for example, it takes one minute to fish a cast out thoroughly, fishing the fly slowly as we normally should, and taking but one pace between casts, a pool the like of Cairnty will take ten hours to cover. Even with four paces between casts, if the pool is fished from neck to tail, the fisherman can still expect to be there for a morning or afternoon. A silly illustration you may say, as we tend to concentrate on those sections most likely to hold fish, but food for thought nevertheless.

What are the great beats of the Lower Spey? One's mind immediately turns to Aikenway, the Brae Water, Delfur or Orton but, for now, let us concentrate on just one. Gordon Castle, beside being perhaps the most famous Spey beat, is also the one closest to the sea. It has as many tales to tell as any, and a great deal more than many.

Only two verified salmon of more than 50lb have been taken from the Spey, besides the monster caught by Duncan Grant, whose exact weight cannot truly be verified. Both the verified fish came from Gordon Castle. Mr W. G. Craven's record Spey salmon has already been mentioned, but only briefly, in the section on the Middle Spey. A brief mention, and a brief fight. The 53lb salmon was ashore in fifteen minutes. How and why was this done? There are many tales of epic struggles with fish half that size in the Spey. The facts were revealed by A. E. Gathorne-Hardy in *The Salmon*, published in 1898, the year after the capture:

> Mr Craven, who was fishing the Dallachy Pool, not more than a mile from the sea, with a small No 4 Carron fly, with lemon body, silver twist and black hackle wing, tied on a double hook, on a double gut cast with four feet of single, observed the fish rising behind a sunken stone and beyond the rapid stream from which he was casting, the rise,

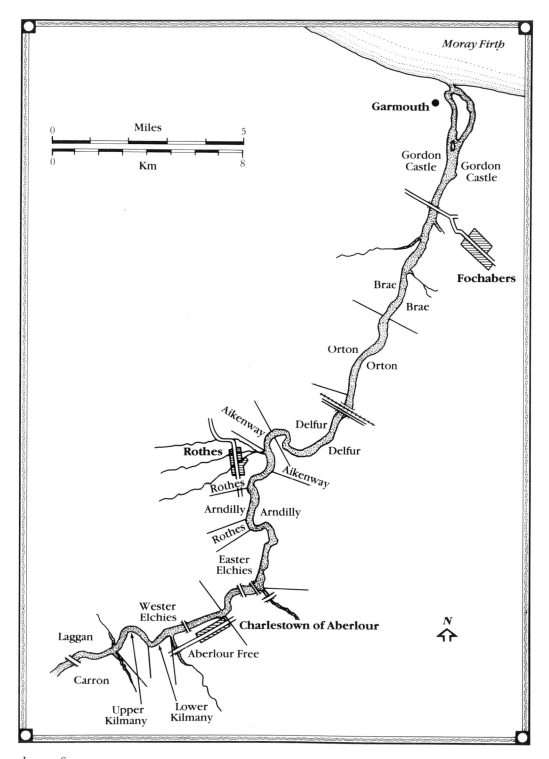

Lower Spey

as is frequently the case with very large fish, being only indicated by the swirl of the water. From this position he could only reach him by casting his fly into the comparatively slack water beyond the stream, and allowing it to be dragged past his nose in a manner quite contrary to the rules of casting. Three times this was done without success, but on the fourth occasion there was a wave on the water and a hard pull, and in a second away went 40 yards of line downstream. Mr Craven was beginning to think of the boat 200 yards below, when the fish suddenly stopped and gave two or three unpleasant tugs; but being very firmly hooked he allowed himself to be reeled slowly up and enabled his captor to get ashore. He then made for his old resting place and began to sulk, but not for long, as he quickly went upstream as fast as he had come down it, and it became a labour of difficulty to keep above him.

At this point a disagreeable grating feeling indicated that the line was rubbing against the edge of the shingle between the rod and the deep water and it was necessary to take to the water again and get the line perpendicularly over him as he again stopped. At this point Mr Craven first realised what a monster he had hooked, for although the rod was apparently pointing directly over the fish, the line suddenly ran out at full speed. This was because having drowned the line under the heavy stream, the salmon was trying to ascend a small 'draw' on the far side of the river and there he showed himself struggling in about eight inches of water. The strong tackle bore the strain well; the sunken part of the line was successfully reeled up and, but for the bend of the rod, the line was once more horizontal between fish and angler. Now a slow, steady pull not only checked his career, but drew him back with a splash into the deep and the line was reeled up short, so that when he had been carried a little way down he came into the slack water, where fisherman and gaffer were waiting for him, but just out of reach. This was repeated twice, but the third time, with two or three more feet reeled up, he came well within reach, and the steel went into him just above the dorsal fin, the left hand came to the rescue of the overtaxed right, and W. Davidson, who had not uttered a syllable during the fifteen minutes contest, broke the silence with the exclamation: 'The biggest fish I have ever taken out of the Spey . . .' His length was four feet one and a half inches, and his girth two feet five; a male fish, rather coloured but in perfect shape and condition. The subsequent examination of the tackle showed that the risk of losing him had been considerable as the reel line was cut a quarter through where it had grated against the shingle, and had to be removed as untrustworthy, and one strand of the double gut eye of the fly was severed and standing out at right angles.

Mr Craven's 53lb salmon was a very unlucky fish indeed. Landing such a fish in the heavy water and strong streams of the Spey would be a difficult enough proposition at any time, let alone on a relatively small hook, with the line damaged, and the gut eye of the old-style fly failing under the enormous pressure. One can only wonder at the outcome of this battle if the salmon had not been unfortunate enough to swim steadily into reach of the gaffer. Gaffs are an emotive subject. Most anglers feel, quite rightly, that they are an unacceptably ignoble end for a truly noble fish. Nevertheless, there is no doubt that they are the best medicine for grassing a salmon of more than 30lb in weight. If ever I was lucky enough to hook such a fish,

Larger Spey pools may be fished from a boat

I would be hoping and praying that some welcome passer-by would be without my own moral scruples and be carrying a gaff.

An example of what can happen when no gaff is available to land a large salmon can be read in Scrope's book, *Days and Nights of Salmon Fishing*:

'Hey mon, sic a fish!'
   He then went for a stone to fell him with; but . . . the fish began to wamble towards the water, and Kerse turned, and jumped upon it; over they both tumbled, and they, hook, line, and all went into the Tweed.

Although the gaff may no longer be popular, it is, as stated, a very great aid to landing the size of fish that most anglers dream of catching; also, it is an interesting piece of fishing tackle from the historical point of view. Nobody can say how far it goes back in history, before the days of rod and line fishing. It would undoubtedly have been used to snatch a fish from its lie close to the bank, or perhaps when leaping a falls.

One of the earliest references to the gaff in the literature of fishing appears in *Barker's Delight* of 1657 where the author advises of the need for 'a good large landing hook' for landing the salmon. Then there is reference to a 'landing rod' in Franck's *Northern Memoirs* of 1658.

In the past, gaffs were certainly in general use on the Spey, and up to fairly recent times were used to grass practically all but grilse. One famed gillie on the Spey was proud of his home-made gaff which had been fashioned out of the tine of a garden fork. The problem was that any fish into the teens of pounds would start to straighten the gape as it was swung ashore, and larger fish could straighten it right out, dropping the fish back into the river. Perhaps the poor man was only trying to be subtle in his desire to be presented with a new and more effective weapon. One wonders whether he ever got one!

Talking specifically of the Gordon Castle Water however, when the Duke of Richmond and Gordon's fishery records were inspected by Calderwood for his book *Salmon Rivers of Scotland*, published at the start of this century, those records revealed, on the fishing as it was then from Boat o' Brig at the bottom of Delfur to the sea, the following catches over a period of ten years:

1890	452	1895	696
1891	899	1896	583
1892	950	1897	495
1893	705	1898	426
1894	813	1899	445

There are an awful lot of rivers, let alone individual beats, that would be proud to boast such salmon catches. And these are just the catch figures for the period of 1 September to 15 October for each year – the period after netting had ceased.

Nowadays, fishing with rod and line on the Spey ends on 30 September so

A lady throwing a good line on Greenbanks on Castle Grant water, under the watchful eye of her gillie

New and old bridges on the Spey at Craigellachie

comparisons cannot clearly be drawn. There are, however, knowledgeable fishermen who say that the catch figures of the end of the last century on Gordon Castle could be equalled in the last six weeks of the current season, although the fish would not be of such a great weight. Last century, the average would have been 16–18lb, and there would have been plenty of 30- and 40-pounders. Today, a 20lb fish would be talked about at dinner, and the average weight would be nearer to 10lb. One day then produced seventy salmon, another showed eighty. To modern sportsmen's eyes, the sight of eighty salmon laid out for inspection might not be considered a worthy thing. At Gordon Castle, however, at the turn of the century, the sight of huge hauls of fish was a regular occurrence. That is why the catch figures given are only for the last six weeks of the season, after netting had ceased. Up to that time, fifteen netting crews rotated to fish the water continuously from the start of the season on 11 February through until 26 August. With only a 42-hour 'slap' period, when nets are not allowed to operate, at weekends, this netting activity almost annihilated the returning runs of Spey salmon. Fortunately, Gordon Castle netting operations ceased entirely in 1903 above Cumberland Ford, just one mile below Fochabers, and more spring and summer fish were allowed to ascend. Today, netting operations on the Spey have been reduced still further, and this in itself is enough to bode well for an even brighter future.

SPEY SEA TROUT

This book is about great salmon beats and fishing. In mentioning the Spey, however, it would seem a crime not to mention the really excellent quality of its sea trout. The Spey is emerging, perhaps, as the greatest sea trout river in Britain. They have always been there, of course, but it seems that for some reason we are now catching far more of them, and sea trout of better quality as well as quantity. At one level, this could be explained by the fact that more fishermen on the river are prepared to try for them deliberately, rather than simply regarding them as a happy extra in the course of trout or salmon fishing. However, it would seem to go a little bit deeper than that. Those who know the Spey and its sea trout say that the present populations contain definite generations of fish. This is what successful sea trout fisheries are all about. Many more sea trout survive the rigours of the spawning run than do salmon, and this leads to multi-return fish. Over the last two decades, more and more of these two- and three-time spawners are being found in the Spey.

The growth rate of Spey sea trout certainly seems to be excellent. I remember a friend calling in for Sunday lunch when we lived in Argyll. He was en route between the Spey and the island of Mull. Scottish migratory fish may not be taken after the witching hour on Saturday night, so I knew that my friend could only have had two hours' fishing, from 10 until midnight, when he asked me to come and see the fish he had caught. Taking his bag out of the boot of his car, he tipped out seven Spey sea trout onto the heather. Their total weight exceeded 30lb. Two hours' sport with the floating line, and the very stuff that a sea trout fisherman's dreams are made of!

Spinning a Spey pool near Fochabers

A very interesting factor emerges in regard to Spey sea trout. You will recall that most of the river's rod-caught salmon come from downstream of Grantown. It is definitely the middle and lower river that yield the best spoort. And yet, for sea trout, it is undoubtedly the upper-middle and upper river, as well as its tributaries the Feshie and Avon, which produce the bulk of the sea-trout catch. One reason for this is that the lower beats are expensive. Perhaps, it is said, the people who can afford the rents may only be interested in salmon. This is not such a silly idea. Top-quality salmon fishing could be said to hold similar appeal to first-class pheasant shooting. Sea trout, on the other hand, particularly as they have a nocturnal habit, could be described as the equivalent of duck and geese. Sea trout, duck and geese – you have to be out and up early to achieve success with any of these species. The flesh is frail, and after a full day's salmon fishing it is hard to raise enthusiasm to return to the river for an all-night sea trout session.

CHAPTER 11

THE ABERDEENSHIRE DEE

There are a number of rivers that are named the Dee in Britain. However, there is but one Aberdeenshire Dee and, as a salmon river as well as a scenic treat, it is quite spectacular. It is little wonder that the Royal Family have maintained Balmoral Castle and its estate, including a beat on the Dee, as their Scottish retreat. For some of them, the time spent at Balmoral is the highlight of their year. Since Queen Victoria and Prince Albert first purchased this estate, the strath has received the Royal stamp of approval, and has come to be widely known as 'Royal Deeside'.

As mentioned earlier, an interesting mark of the gillies' character is the unwritten code they follow in regard to their relations with the Royals. No gillie worthy of the name would ever discuss their doings, and this tradition has continued into the time when the modern 'paparazzi' of the world, ever eager for a 'scoop', have brought the methods of inducement and hounding to a science. Indeed, Balmoral locals can even point out the places where patient cameramen will find a vantage point, as close to the castle as they are allowed to get, with high-powered lenses trained and waiting to get a picture of those entering or leaving the castle. For the fisherman, however, there are far better things to look at in the area.

In many ways the Dee is similar to the Spey. Both present near-ideal conditions for fishing the fly, being relatively fast-flowing. In the spring and early summer, with both having sources in the high Cairngorms, water levels are maintained by a steady snow melt. The Dee, however, whilst undoubtedly being fast-flowing compared with many rivers, is unlike the Spey in that it has the standard gradient common to most rivers – that is, steepest in its upper reaches, softening in its middle section and finally

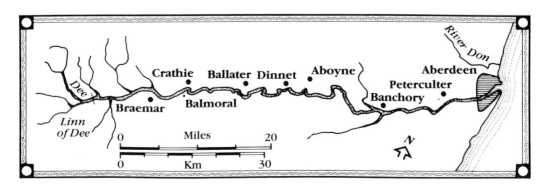

The Aberdeenshire Dee

flowing through gentler, arable country on the final part of its journey to the sea at Aberdeen.

The Dee is roughly 90 miles in length from its principal sources on Ben Macdhui and Braeriach, both at a height of about 4,000ft. Upper Dee can provide some excellent sport, but it is really the bottom 60 miles that represent the classic section of the river, from Peterculter up to Dinnet and Glen Tanar. Incidentally, the recognised source of the Dee is regarded as the Wells of Dee. The burn from here tumbles down to the Lairig Ghru which is a popular pass with hill-walkers travelling from Deeside to Speyside. It is, in fact, this Lairig Burn and the Gharbh Choire Burn which meet at the foot of Cairn Toul from where the flow is recognised as the River Dee, flowing through Glen Dee. Some miles downstream it reaches the Linns of Dee, a series of waterfalls which tend to halt the passage of fish if there is insufficient water. The ranks of salmon lying in the crystal clear waters of the cavernous pools below the falls are a great tourist attraction. Sometimes, in their eagerness and excitement, these folk get a little too close to the edge. Last year I was fishing there, perched high on a rocky ledge with my fly working the water some thirty feet below. Some children were getting too adventurous on the opposite rock face, and I called over to them to be careful. As I looked back at my fly, it was dangling a foot or two above the water, and the silvery flank of a raised salmon turned beneath it, put off by the long Collie Dog suddenly becoming airborne. I had been covering those fish for hours without moving a fin, and a few seconds' lack of attention caused me to miss that fish. Oh well, such is salmon fishing! The beats on this part of the river are Mar Lodge on the left bank, and Mar Estate on the right. Incidentally, in case you are not aware of the fact, references to right or left bank are given when facing in a downstream direction.

Between the Linns and the village of Braemar, another tourist attraction and home of a famous Highland Games, is a distance of about 8 miles. Downstream from Braemar is perhaps the most scenically attractive section of the river, through a pine-clad gentle glen, passing through Invercauld Estate and Balmoral and on to Brig o' Dee. Before the river reaches Ballater, it is joined by four important tributaries. These are the Gelder and Girnock Burns, which are near Crathie, and the River Gairn and the Muick, both of which are important spawning tributaries. Upstream of Ballater, besides Balmoral and Invercauld, other good salmon beats include Abergeldie and Birkhall.

The Dee flows swiftly from Ballater to Aboyne. If one had to choose three beats on which to fish in this area, the names of Cambus o' May, Glen Tanar and Birse Castle would immediately spring to mind. Aboyne Castle is another splendid beat. It has been time-shared, however, and tends therefore to be closed for short-term access. What marvellous pools there are on this beat! The Red Rock is perhaps the most interesting of all, with its very narrow neck and extremely fast broken stream on the cheeks of which many a salmon and grilse has been found. The current runs on through the pool before striking the red rocks on the south bank which deflect the force of the current back out into the tail of the pool. Quite intriguing, and a

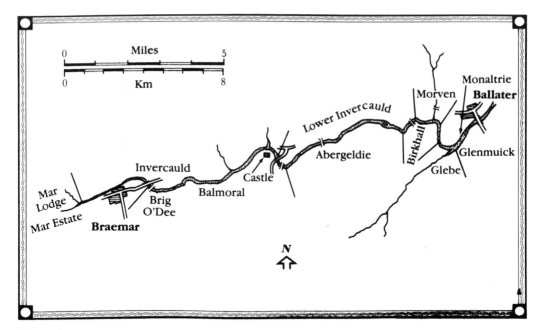

Upper Dee

challenge to fish well with the fly. And as for the force of the stream up in the head of the pool, well, it takes a steady wader just to get his knees wet!

From Aboyne to Banchory, the Dee continues to offer outstanding fishing. Among the best of the beats in this area are Dess, Carlogie, Ballogie, Woodend, Cairnton, Inchmarlo and Blackhall. Incidentally, it was on Cairnton that Arthur Wood perfected his greased-line technique of salmon fishing. This is fully described in Chapter 6 on warm water tactics, for spring and summer. Sceptics as to the high degree of confidence placed by Wood's disciples in the great man's tackle and techniques will no doubt be amused to hear the following little tale.

Those familiar with Wood's teaching will recall that he stated that he placed great faith in a small Blue Charm fly and this, certainly, was the one that was publicised. One evening, when Wood's gillie was enjoying a dram in a local pub, he was approached by the gillie of a neighbouring beat. He wanted to know if this fly might improve his own gentleman's chances. 'Don't you believe it', was the reply. 'It's a great big Jock Scott that is killing all Mr Wood's fish!' Or so the story goes.

Incidentally, another gillie's tale from this area clearly indicates the sort of thing that some of them had to put up with in the days when the laird's word was, almost literally, the law. A certain lord had come to fish. The weather was bad, and the lord, presumably in a light-hearted way, said to his gillie that he could have managed to provide a better day than this. The gillie, with his guard down, replied: 'It was fine enough yesterday. Perhaps you brought it yourself, my lord'. This conversation was reported as a case of insolence. The very next day, the gillie was summoned to the estate factor's office and given his notice.

Fishing the famous Red Rock Pool at Aboyne

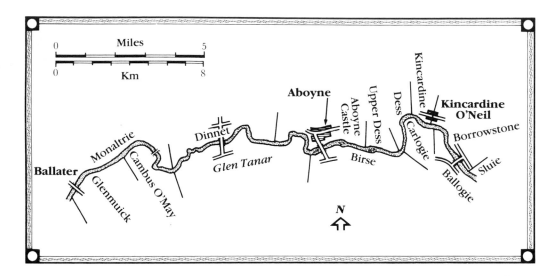

Middle Dee

To return to Arthur Wood, he rented the Cairnton fishing from 1913 to 1934, and the title 'Arthur Wood of Cairnton' was a homage paid by fishermen of the time who adopted his technique. It also hints at something else because, so far as can be established he did practically no fishing except on this beat. One would expect that this might create a rather blinkered view of salmon fishing and little awareness of the great diversity of sport enjoyed throughout the long British salmon season on a full range of rivers from the cosy and intimate little streams right through to the pomp and majesty of the mightiest of classic rivers. It has already been said that Cairnton is one of two Dee beats that can virtually be fished with a fly without the angler needing to wet his boots. In hindsight, it is a matter for some wonderment that a technique based on such a narrow field of experience, not to mention such a non-typical beat, should ever have caught on. But it did, and how! No secret was made of the fact that, during his 21 years on the beat, Arthur Wood killed 3,490 salmon – an average in excess of 150 fish each season. However, such things have to be put into context, and it is interesting to read what John Ashley Cooper said in *The Great Salmon Rivers of Scotland* in regard to Wood's catch record:

> . . . is it such a vast total, considering that Cairnton was reputed to be, in those days, one of the best holding beats on the Dee, and that Mr Wood is said to have reserved the Grey Mare, one of the best pools, entirely for his own use?

Having reported that, there is no doubt that Wood was a fine fisherman. One wonders, however, how much better he might have done if he had not insisted on a 12ft rod and those now virtually ignored long-shanked single hooks. Still, it must give him a chuckle now and then to look down and see that we are all still talking about him!

Lest anybody should harbour ideas that Wood's design of long-shanked, low-water, single hooks are anything but the poorest of hookers and holders, despite what Wood insisted to the contrary, he need only refer to the following rather self-incriminating passage from Anthony Crossley's book, *The Floating Line for Salmon and Sea Trout*, published at the start of World War II. In it he states:

> In April and May 1931 A.H.W. (Arthur Wood) met 336 at Cairnton and killed 179. In March, April and May, I met 323 at Careysville, Cairnton and Tulchan and killed 176. In both cases these were all killed on single hooks.

The results are remarkably consistent. Using their single hooks, neither Wood nor Crossley, both experienced fishermen, were able to grass more than half the fish that they raised to their flies. Today, in an age of wee doubles and tiny trebles on the great salmon beats for summer work, most fishermen would be tearing their hair out at such a poor result. No, unfortunately it was one of the very men who championed the long-shanked singles who, in the end, provided the unarguable evidence as to its ineffective nature when it came to the hooking and holding of salmon.

Let that not detract, however, from the best of Wood's technique. It was he, above all others, who showed other fishermen the technique of mending line, and started so many salmon fishermen thinking positively in terms of controlling the speed and angle of the fly fished off a floating line and, indeed, the sinker.

Having passed below Banchory, there is still another 20 miles of Dee to be fished before it enters the sea. Most of the best beats on the Dee are single-bank fishing. This is certainly true of the lower section with great beats such as Crathes, Drum and Park on the left bank and Durris, Tilbourie and Altries on the right. Out of a total of 45 recognised beats, 39 have just one side of the river. Admittedly, some proprietors have made arrangements to obtain at least some of the fishing from the opposite bank or, in other cases, mutually satisfactory arrangements and agreements have been reached. Nevertheless, most of the river remains single-bank fishing and this can, inevitably, lead to some degree of friction when you are dependent on

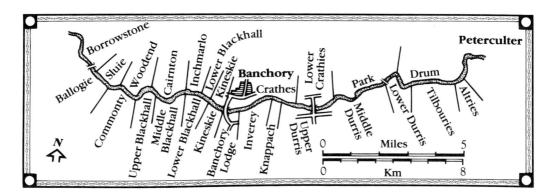

Lower Dee

nothing more than a gentleman's agreement and code of conduct when, whatever else the party fishing the other bank may be, they are certainly not 'gentlemen'. What to do in such a situation? It can be very difficult indeed. The last time I fished a Dee beat all our party were fishing the fly. It was, after all, at the end of May. However, we were faced with a barrage of prawns and spinners flying out towards us from the opposite shore. As it happened, the opposite party were very considerate and well-mannered about the whole thing, always giving way to us fly fishermen, with a smile and a wave. And yet, despite what anybody might say, it knocks the heart out of a fly fishermen to fish through a pool which has just been covered with a spinner or, even worse, a prawn. So they fished, smiled and waved, while we suffered with the best grace we could muster. They seemed far too pleasant a group to get particularly angry with. Incidentally, the rule on the Dee, although it was flouted in this case, is a gentleman's agreement that you can fish fly or spin (not bait) up until mid-April. After that, except in high water when some beats are happy to allow spinning, the agreement is fly-only.

The great beats mentioned above lie in the upper part of this lower section. The seven miles of the Dee that lie closest to the sea are picturesque as they flow through park lands and tree-lined banks and on through the populated area of Aberdeen but, from a fishing point of view, certainly in regard to great salmon beats, are not comparable to the rest of the river.

So there we have a whistle-stop tour of the Dee from source to sea. It has been far too fast, however, to describe the river, its beats, and the quite outstanding quality of its fishing. The first thing one notes about the Dee, and upon which all fishermen will comment, is the clarity of the water. To say that the waters of the Dee run gin-clear except in the wake of a spate is not to overstate the case. Wading chest-deep, you can see every rock, pebble and almost grain of sand for a good distance all round. Only the Avon, tributary of the Spey, rivals the Dee in this respect, certainly within Scotland.

Then there is an almost 'fairy-tale' quality to the river and its surroundings. Travelling from neighbouring Don to the Dee, you cross the summit at the watershed between Gairn Shiel and Crathie. The view stretches out before you over the Dee valley and on to the haunting presence of the immense massif of Lochnagar. Lochnagar, the 'Loch of Laughter', inspired HRH Prince Charles to write a children's story called *The Old Man of Lochnagar* which was not only published but also narrated by a kilted Prince high on the Deeside hills before television cameras. One turns from Lochnagar to the view of distant Ben Avon and the Cairngorms. Indeed, you could spend so much time drinking in the sights, scents and sounds of Deeside that there would be little time left for the fishing. What a tragedy that might be, for there is a never-ending procession of some of the most exciting and varied pools to be enjoyed where the clear champagne of water bubbles over rock and gravel before rushing on through the rapid runs.

To list these pools would be an exciting but perhaps pointless task, filling at least two pages of this book. A few must be included, however. Invercauld, on the opposite bank to Balmoral, has Clachanrar, Polslake, Weaver, Cairnaquheen, Upper Boat Pool, Clerach, Geordie Mitchell, Castle, Laundry Pool, Polmonier and Skolpach as representative of the upper river. But no, we won't go on for there must be close to a hundred more pools before reaching Aboyne, and that is barely half-way to Drum Water and Peterculter.

The thing about these pools, all the way down the Dee, is that they offer such a great variety. The Dee is rightly considered a medium-sized river, but that is not to say that there are not plenty of pools to test the casting skills and deep wading abilities of even polished performers. Indeed, there are some pools on the lower river where the fishermen, in order to cover the water completely and effectively, must resort to a boat. Contrast this with beats such as Cairnton where there is seldom any need to wade deeper than knee-height. As mentioned earlier, Arthur Wood fished this beat very largely off the bank or man-made croys.

In regard to the Dee and its season of salmon fishing, it is very significant that there are no artificial obstructions to the passage of fish, absolutely none. This really is very important because, in the case of a number of other rivers discussed in this book, we have seen that the effect of, for example, damming and harnessing a river for hydro-electricity is that there is an immediate tendency for early season spring runs to dwindle to near extinction in favour of summer salmon and grilse. It seems that springers must have free and easy access to the headwaters of a river system if they are to spawn and prosper in sufficient numbers to make their pursuit a worthwhile proposition. Rivers on the east coast of Scotland north of Inverness have, in a number of cases, suffered very badly in this respect. On the Dee, however, the first obstacle encountered by salmon as they move upstream are the Linns of Dee, which are only a stone's throw short of 80 miles upstream from the mouth of the river. Even the Linn is not impassable to fish. Salmon are taken upstream of this series of falls, on the Mar water, but only after May and when there has been a good flow of water to encourage the salmon through. And so salmon returning to the Dee have free passage to all the main river's spawning redds, which are extensive, as well as all its major spawning tributaries. This in itself is not, perhaps, sufficient to ensure the early runs of salmon into the Dee. For example, it is quite clear that high-sea netting, while apparently making a not too significant inroad into summer grilse stocks, has without a doubt created havoc with spring stocks. It is assumed that the ocean feeding grounds of mature salmon are the ones that have been discovered by the world's fishing fleets while those of grilse remain something of a secret. Equally, spring salmon are in the river for the greatest length of time before spawning and are, therefore, not only subject to losses brought about by rod and line fishing but also the far more devastating activities of organised and ruthless poaching gangs operating with explosives, poisons and nets. Give the Dee's spring salmon a chance, however, and their parent river has the ability to cater to their needs.

River Avon, Hampshire. A fresh-run salmon, weighing 15lb, caught by ninety-year-old Clifford Spital at Avon Tyrell near Ringwood

Deep wading and long casting during the early months of the Dee season

A 34lb cock fish caught below Ringwood on the River Avon

Talking about the nature of pools on the Dee, its potential for the extensive provision of spawning redds, and touching upon one aspect of management, all leads into another characteristic of the Dee. It contains a tremendous amount of gravel. At one level, purely from the practical fisherman's point of view, this certainly leads to easy, pleasant wading. Gravel, as we know, is also required for the salmon in which to create their spawning redds. However, the Dee, like any river, is subject to spates. At times, these can be very heavy, and they can be sudden with a viciously fast run-off. It is an expensive but fairly simple matter to protect river banks in order to prevent erosion. It is far more difficult to control the movement of gravel. Remember that salmon have a preference for pools containing rocks and boulders as they like nothing better than finding some small nook where they can lie with their bellies pressed onto a slab of flat rock. Many a good holding pool has been ruined when gravel has been set on the move by a big spate. Practically overnight, all the attractive holding lies in a pool can be covered in gravel to a depth of several inches or more and, unless that gravel is swept away, salmon will continue, season after season, to seek out alternative accommodation. Therefore, on the Dee and other rivers where this has shown itself to be a problem, stone or concrete groynes have been constructed to affect and control gravel movement.

Returning to the theme of the Dee salmon, it is true that they are small fish, on average, and yet there will always be some large fish along with them. Fifty-pounders may have been very scarce, but then that is true of the great majority of rivers, and this lack, if so it can be called, is more than made up for by a smattering of 40-pounders. The record salmon for the Dee was a salmon of either 56 or 57½lb – accounts vary – caught by J. Gordon, the gillie on Ardoe Water. It met its end in October 1886. The runner-up is a salmon of 52lb, caught by M. Ewen in October 1918 at Park. It may be noted that both these fish came from lower Dee beats. Park is sandwiched between Lower Crathes and Drum. Ardoe is still further downstream, between Altries and Aberdeen. What is even more interesting is that both these fish were killed in the autumn. In the modern age, the Dee has come to be regarded as almost exclusively a spring and summer proposition. And yet, could it be that the Dee may once again be establishing an autumn run of fish? There have certainly been rumours from lower beats that they have experienced runs of fresh fish at the back-end of the season, and I am hoping that I may get a practical opportunity to judge the truth behind this later in the present season of 1989.

This possibility of an autumn run into the Dee raises all sorts of questions. It can only be hoped that, if it is true, these runs will be in addition, rather than as a replacement, to the springers of the opening months of the season. Heavy runs of late summer and autumn fish are not unknown to the Dee, of course. Ernest Crosfield killed eleven salmon, the largest being a 30-pounder and the average weight 23lb on Park in October 1918 – the same beat, month and year as M. Ewen's salmon of 52lb. Then there was Major J. L. Dickie who in his book *Forty Years of Trout and Salmon Fishing* described frequently catching fresh run salmon on the Dee in October during the 1880s.

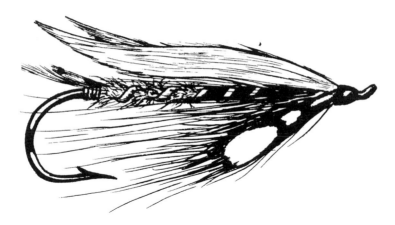

'Ackroyd'. A Dee 'strip wing' fly with the Jungle Cock cheek set below the line of the hook shank and heron hackle. Invented by Charles Ackroyd circa 1880, and while such traditionals maintained their popularity it was a great slayer of salmon

It is interesting that none of the salmon just mentioned, neither the record fish of Messrs Gordon and Ewen nor the catches of Ernest Crosfield and Major Dickie, could be caught today. It would be illegal. The rod season now closes on 30 September.

Whatever the past, present and future of autumn fishing in the Dee may be, however, this should not take away from the fact that it is still an outstanding spring river and, in a time when most rivers are experiencing meagre early season fishing, this fact sets it apart in terms of Scottish salmon rivers. Fish run the Dee far earlier than the Spey. Where these early salmon will be found depends on the climate of the year. Remember that at the opening of the season, the height of the Dee water is very dependent on the amount of snow melt on the high mountains and corries that are the river's place of birth. When the Dee season opens on 1 February, so much depends on the nature of the winter. If it has been cold and hard, salmon will prefer to rest in the lower sections of the river, certainly downstream of Banchory. There they will stay until the water warms considerably. On the heels of a hard winter, this may not be until well into April.

A mild winter, on the other hand, will raise the water levels, and fish will run beyond Banchory and might be found as high as Invercauld on the opening day. One man's gain is another man's loss, and one can understand that upper beat proprietors are not too unhappy to see the snow melt starting early. But this is rare, and the general pattern of spring fishing is that beats below Banchory enjoy the cream of the sport from the opening of the season up until some time in April although fish will have started to ease up towards Ballater from mid-March, giving good fishing there from that time until mid-May. Upstream of Ballater, the best sport cannot be expected before the period of early May to the end of June.

I experienced a clear-cut example of the nature of Dee salmon runs when fishing up at Mar. The time of season was May, and we knew that although there were very

A late springer coming to the net

few fish in the beat, enormous runs and great sport had been enjoyed as far upstream as Aboyne, where the salmon seemed to have stuck. On the Tuesday evening, our prayers for rain were finally answered. It was not a great deluge but, coupled with a short burst of snow melt, the upper Dee rose nearly a foot and the temperature dropped from the lower fifties to the lower forties. We were up at daybreak, four hours before civilised man would contemplate breakfast, and down on the river. We had several hours to wait, and then the vanguard of the Aboyne fish, running for the Linns, began to trickle and then flow into the beat. We were lucky enough to get among them.

Lower Dee fishermen may tend to write off some of the uppermost beats, but every dog has his day and while the upper river may never equal the catches of its fatter cousins, sport up to the Linns can be spectacular. There is royal testimony to the quality of Dee sport even above the Linns, once salmon have had the necessary height of water to ease their passage through this system of waterfalls and cauldron pools. W. L. Calderwood, Inspector of Salmon Fisheries for Scotland at the start of the century, reported that HRH Princess Louise, sister of King George V, had twelve salmon in a day, and that barely eleven miles below the Wells of Dee, source of the river.

In terms of sheer numbers alone, it is fairly safe to say that the Dee produces spring salmon fishing that is second to none in Britain or indeed the world. Despite rumours of autumn runs on some lower beats, the evidence from most Dee beats seems to suggest that the quantity of the spring catch may be, if anything, on the increase.

Following these spring runs, the number of fish entering the river, in comparative terms, starts to dwindle. That is not to say that there are no summer runs. The Dee can show good sport with grilse and, now that netting activities have ceased, the beats are waiting to see how much of a difference this will make in the long term. In terms of the enhancement of salmon stocks, one swallow should never be seen to herald the coming of summer and it will be a few years yet before anybody can make more than guarded suggestions as to any change in trends emerging from fish at all times of the season obtaining free passage. As they say, time alone will truly tell.

It is worth noting that after the fairly steady upstream migration of early season fish – their progress up river having already been charted – the bulk of later arrivals seem keener to travel long and hard, with parcels of fish passing quickly through the lower and middle beats. At this time, the old axiom of 'make hay while the sun shines' should be borne in mind by the Dee fisherman.

CHAPTER 12

THE TAY

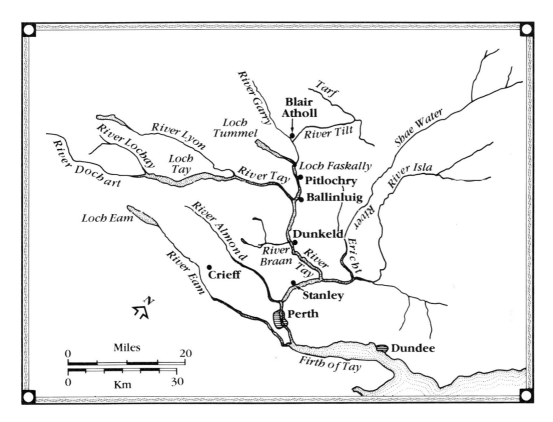

The Tay system

The River Almond, a tributary of the Tay. Where a major tributary joins the principal river is often a fine place for excellent sport with salmon, as on Almondmouth and, further upstream, Islamouth

The Tay is the largest river in Scotland. It is often referred to as the greatest salmon river of them all. Describing its fishing and its great salmon beats, not to mention its tributaries Almond, Dochart, Garry, Isla, Lochy, Lyon and Tummel, in any sort of detail could fill each and every page of this book.

The Tay is 123 miles long, shorter than a river like the Wye of the English/Welsh borderlands, but having a catchment area estimated at the enormous amount of 2,400 square miles. It is said to be the one salmon river to have fresh fish entering it, swimming up through the Firth of Tay past Dundee and on to Perth, during each and every week of the season. This bald statement, however, should not blind us to the true picture of Tay salmon runs. Until recently famed as a producer of spring salmon, the Tay is showing a distinct tendency towards late summer and autumn runs. Longstanding visitors to Tay beats are, in many cases, abandoning the river in the early part of the season, from 15 January, and seeking out the availability of weeks at the back end, up to the close of the Tay season on 15 October. Having made that point, all hope that the Tay will return to its spring glories through netting control and, therefore, in this chapter we shall be looking at the traditional as well as the current scene.

I have mentioned the tributaries, at least the principal ones, of the Tay. As salmon rivers in their own right, they are worthy of attention. Equally, they can strongly influence the fishing at least in parts of the main river. What tributaries would the Tay salmon encounter after passing Perth on its journey to the headwaters and Loch Tay?

Just above Perth is the Almond, flowing north-east into the main river from Glen Almond and parallel to Strath Earn. Incidentally, the Earn is accepted as a river in its own right, rather than a Tay tributary, as it joins the Tay below Perth, in tidal waters. To return to the Almond, this tributary carries a run of summer salmon and grilse. Surprisingly perhaps, when one considers its proximity to tidal waters, despite the large numbers of early season fish that must pass it as they enter the Tay the Almond has never had a reputation as a producer of early season fish. The junction pool, however, formed by the confluence of Almond with Tay waters and known as Almondmouth, has long had a reputation for producing salmon from the opening day of the season.

Moving upstream, the next tributary of note is the Isla, which flows in from the north to join the Tay at Cargill. At one time, salmon running the Isla would be stopped at Cargill's Leap, close to Blairgowrie. This was a fall that salmon would not ascend until times of warmer water: in other words, a temperature pool existed below the Leap. The solution was found in a stick of dynamite. The falls were blown, and early running salmon gained immediate access to the Isla and its tributary the Ericht. Spring salmon fishing may not be so worthy of note today, but time was when it was reported that an individual member of the Blairgowrie Angling Club had about a hundred salmon to his own rod between the opening of the season and May.

As at Almondmouth, and on so many junction pools, the confluence of the Isla with the Tay produces a fine holding pool. Try to find out just how many salmon are caught on Islamouth, and you will come up against a wall of silence. However, I have been told in the past that the total is into four figures and it is a widely held opinion that Islamouth may well be the most prolific salmon pool to be found anywhere in Scotland. Tweedsiders might argue for the Junction of Tweed and Teviot, but there we are.

Travelling on up the Tay to Dunkeld, the main river is joined by the Bran. This looks like an excellent little salmon river, except for the fact that there are insurmountable falls at the Hermitage, about one mile up from the Tay. It is only in this short, lower section that the Bran can produce salmon.

At Blairgowrie, the waters of the Tummel and its tributaries Garry, Tilt and Tarf join the Tay. It is at Pitlochry that fish running the Tay and into the Tummel meet a major obstacle to their progress. This is Pitlochry Dam with its fish ladder and viewing gallery. Thousands of tourists stop each year to gaze at salmon ascending the fish ladder. Swimming behind reinforced glass windows set in the side of the ladder, mighty salmon and slender grilse hold station, so close that you feel you can reach out and touch them. It is a sight that I remember from early childhood days, one that perhaps stirred my lifelong interest in salmon and fishing, and to which I have returned on many occasions. Most salmon, however, instead of running the Tummel, turn west at Ballinluig, staying with the main river up to Loch Tay. In the area of the loch there are three more tributaries – the Lyon just below the loch and the Lochay and Dochart above it.

There we have a brief description of the Tay and its major tributaries. Just how great a salmon river is it? Well, great it certainly is, but it is hard even to guestimate its total catches over the years, divided between rod and net. Nobody has a vested interest in revealing exact figures for a beat, unless, of course, it is to be sold. This is very understandable at one level, although it does little to ease the burden of those charged with ensuring the well being of the river and its salmon. For example, most Tay regulars assert that early season catches are well down but, accepting this to be true, by how much, what percentage, and are the fish running later, being intercepted or what?

UPPER TAY

It is strange but true that the Tay is recognised as starting at the outflow from Loch Tay. Strange, because above Loch Tay is the River Dochart and the Fillan Water. These flow into Loch Tay, which is a large sheet of water about fifteen miles long and almost one mile wide. It is below this loch, where the flow is already substantial, that the Tay itself is recognised as such, and from the outflow of Loch Tay at Kenmore and down to the confluence with the Tummel at Ballanluig can be fairly considered as upper Tay.

This section may be classified for the sake of convenience as upper river but, make no mistake, here is no small stream. It may be relatively small compared with the fatter beats of the middle and lower river but, in Highland terms, the upper Tay is

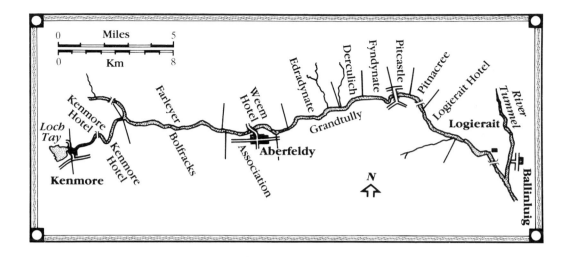

Upper Tay

a substantial flow. It has a charming atmosphere and offers good fishing prospects on tumbling, rocky stretches that fish the fly well. Grandtully is one beat that is particularly notable in this respect – other beats may have stretches on them that are too slow to be of great interest interspersed in their more exciting stretches. Besides Grandtully, perhaps the best known of upper Tay beats, working down from Kenmore are Taymouth Castle, Farleyer, Fyndynate and Logierait. Other beats in the area include Bolfracks, Weem Hotel Water, Edradynate, Derculich, Pitcastle and Pitnacree and Kinnaird, which extends below the junction with the Tummel.

Returning to Loch Tay, it was described by Sir John Murray in his *Bathymetrical Survey of the Fresh Water Lochs of Scotland* as 'unsurpassed in the beauty of its surroundings, and well known to anglers on account of its salmon fishings, which are among the best in Scotland'. It is a deep loch, having an average depth of 200ft, and for this reason among others it is normally fished with lures such as the Toby Spoon and Rapala, trailed behind a boat. In the old days, when about twenty boats fished it intensively, the Loch Tay season would produce in the region of five hundred salmon. Nowadays, surprisingly in an age of ever increasing demand for salmon fishing, there are fewer boats fishing the loch. Equally, there are fewer knowledgeable local gillies to take out guests. Today, it is a rare season when the catch exceeds three hundred salmon.

A fine tradition of salmon fishing is maintained at Kenmore on the opening day of the season when a piper leads the fishermen down to the loch, where a boat is blessed by having a bottle of Scotland's finest cracked over the bows. Thankfully, after all this pomp and ceremony, it is normal for at least one fisherman to return with a salmon at the end of the day.

Even in its upper stretches, the Tay remains a substantial size – the Kinnaird water near Ballinluig

MIDDLE TAY

Kinnaird spans the junction between upper Tay and middle Tay, and middle Tay can fairly be taken as extending from there down to Islamouth below Meikleour. Obviously, once Tay has been joined by Tummel, the river becomes a bigger proposition. The pools become both deeper and longer and, therefore, boat fishing as opposed to wading becomes more of a necessity. Wading will cover some of the water of course, but not all of it although, as everywhere, salmon show their preference for rocky bottomed pools and faster, broken water, leaving much of the slower, deeper parts of the river untenanted. Middle Tay beats that are particularly good for showing sport in their time are Dalguise, Glendelvine, Kinnaird and Murthly.

Glendelvine was the scene of the hooking, epic struggle and final capture of the British record salmon by Miss Georgina Ballantine on 7 October 1922. Georgina Ballantine was the daughter of James Ballantine, who was gillie to Sir Alexander Lyle,

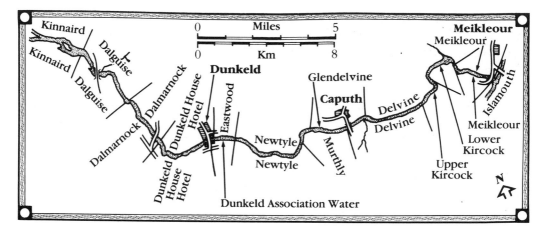

Middle Tay

the Laird of Glendelvine. On the day in question she had already caught three fine salmon in the morning – fish of 17, 21 and 25lb which, when one sees a photograph of the young, slimly built Georgina might, you would think, have provided enough excitement and exertion for one day. However, father and daughter decided to go out in the evening for an hour's harling.

Harling is a productive if not very demanding form of fishing as practised on the Tay. Basically, the method relies on a lure or lures being allowed to trail behind the boat while the boatman rows slowly back and forth across the pool, allowing the boat to slip a little further downstream on each bank-to-bank sweep. The skill, it has to be said, is all with the boatman, the angler being required to do little besides hooking and playing the fish.

Harling may be carried out with three rods but, on this occasion, the Ballantines decided to fish with two. The split-cane rod was chosen to fish a Wilkinson fly. A heavy greenheart rod would carry the dace, a revolving lure of mottled brown appearance.

It was 6.15 in the evening when the trailing dace was taken away with a real bang. It is said that the force of that initial impact very nearly tore the big greenheart rod from Georgina's grasp. Meanwhile, old James Ballantine was holding the boat steady and reeling up the Wilkinson to clear the decks for action. They were under no illusions at this stage. As Georgina said, she knew 'there was something very, very heavy on'. The salmon proceeded to lead them a merry dance, sweeping back and forth across the river in fifty-yard rushes (the Tay is roughly sixty yards wide at this point). A moment of great trauma came when the salmon lunged into a deep lie behind a rock, but the boat was manoeuvred quickly downstream to prevent the line being rubbed and frayed. The fish shot off again, heading downstream and towing Ballantines and boat down to a point opposite their cottage.

By now the last light of the autumn evening had faded away. Mrs Ballantine was down at the river, lantern in hand, and her daughter and husband were able to shout

out what was happening. Mrs Ballantine's feelings at that point are not recorded, but she would perhaps have realised at hearing the strain in their voices what the true position was. And she would know that Caputh bridge was just one hundred yards below their cottage.

The bridge has two pilings. The Ballantines, in their boat, were hugging the left bank when the salmon made a determined bid to cross the river. It seemed that this was an end to it. Georgina, however, piled on the pressure just as much as she dared and turned the fish to slip between the pilings, where her father could row frantically in its wake.

At this point, I should point out that few salmon fishermen have any conception of the strain involved in playing a fish of this size and energy. Only big game fishermen can realise the gut-aching strain on arms and back. It is said that by this stage Georgina was ready to drop. Totally exhausted, she must have known that whatever reserves of energy she had were fast sapping away. Her father, however, would not touch the rod. He knew what was at stake, or at least suspected it. But young Georgina had been fighting the fish for two long hours.

Then the tide of events began to turn. Georgina was reeling in on a brutally taut line and knew at that moment that she was getting the upper hand. The searing runs of the great salmon had faded away to short bursts. Soon they were over the fish, with the humming line dropping vertically. Anybody who has tried to gaff a big salmon after dark will know that their problems were far from ended.

James set the gaff against the line and slipped it slowly down, searching to feel the knot of the leader. He had made up the leader himself; he knew how many blood knots had been used in its construction. The gaff head slipped down the taut line: one knot, two, three, four and five. He pushed down, turning the gaff, then swept it up. At this stage, accounts differ. Some say James drew the mighty salmon inboard with one enormous heave. The truth seems to be, however, that he was understandably unprepared for the full weight of the fish and let gaff and fish slip from his grasp, but quickly took up a second gaff to complete the task. What an incredible moment of high drama!

Even then, the fish still had some fight in it. Georgina was later interviewed by *The Field* magazine and stated that the salmon was leaping and flapping so much that 'Father thought it was going to jump back in the river and threw himself on top of it'. And what of Georgina? 'My whole arm felt paralysed, and I was so utterly exhausted I could have lain down beside the fish and slept.' It is said that once home and put to bed, she repeatedly suffered nightmares, clutching the brass railings of her bedstead as she had clung to the rod that afternoon.

When she awoke, her name was famous throughout the land. Newspapers throughout Britain carried the news of Georgina's salmon: Weight 64lb; length 54in; girth 28½in. Subsequently, the laird Sir Alexander Lyle gifted the salmon to the Perth Royal Infirmary, after it had lain in state in the window of Malloch's tackle shop in Perth for admiring crowds to come and pay homage. Georgina could not resist joining the crowds and told *The Field* about the following conversation.

I went round to the back and stood for a moment beside two old chaps with white side-whiskers. One said to the other 'A woman? Nae woman ever took a fish like that oot of the water, mon, I would need a horse, a block and tackle, tae tak a fish like that oot. A woman – that's a lee anyway!' I had a quiet chuckle up my sleeve and ran to catch the bus.

Georgina Ballantine knew that it was no lie. And, it is said, her arms remained swollen for two weeks to prove it.

What makes this record salmon perhaps all the more interesting is that it was taken from the middle Tay. In a list of twenty-three salmon weighing over 50lb caught in the river, only three are from this section. These are Georgina's fish, a 52-pounder caught at Kinnaird in 1917, and another Kinnaird salmon weighing 50lb caught by Miss Lettice Ward. In the part of this book devoted to the Wye I have discussed this phenomenon of the ladies, who represent what still must be a tiny minority of anglers, seeming to have this ability for tempting the largest fish. Miss Lettice Ward took her salmon on fly, but whether it was cast or harled, it has been impossible to ascertain.

This middle section of the Tay not only sees the transformation from a medium sized to a large river at the joining with Tummel, but also the flow of the river out of a highland setting and into a wide, rich and arable strath, leaving the hills behind. The water does not lose its impetus, however and, although the enormity of the Tay means that harling or spinning remain the favoured methods, there are some good prospects for fishing the fly. Islamouth has strong, streamy water.

When I first fished the Tay it would have been something of a gillie's joke to announce that you intended to concentrate on fly, certainly downstream of Kinnaird. Nowadays, thanks measurably to the development of carbon-fibre as a rod building material, Tay beats do see more fly fishing. It is, however, Tay fly fishing in a style and character all of its own. My longest rod at the present time is a 17-footer, and this is rightly regarded as an enormous length on most Scottish rivers. And so I couldn't help laughing at the gillie's pronouncement, on a Tay beat that I was fishing for the first time, that 'That's a grand wee rod,' and he meant it. Himself, he used a 20-footer to cast a truly amazing length of line and backing, and this in high summer. Still, the truth of the matter is that you really do need rods in the 16–20ft range in order to approach covering the fat Tay beats effectively; these or a spinning rod.

LOWER TAY

Lower Tay has a characteristic which is reminiscent of the lower Wye: it may be running clear in its middle and upper sections but have risen in a dirty spate on lower beats. In both cases, it is due to the contributory effects of the tributaries. A

(Overleaf) *Playing a February Tay salmon on fly – but spinning and harling are the general rule during cold water times on the Tay*

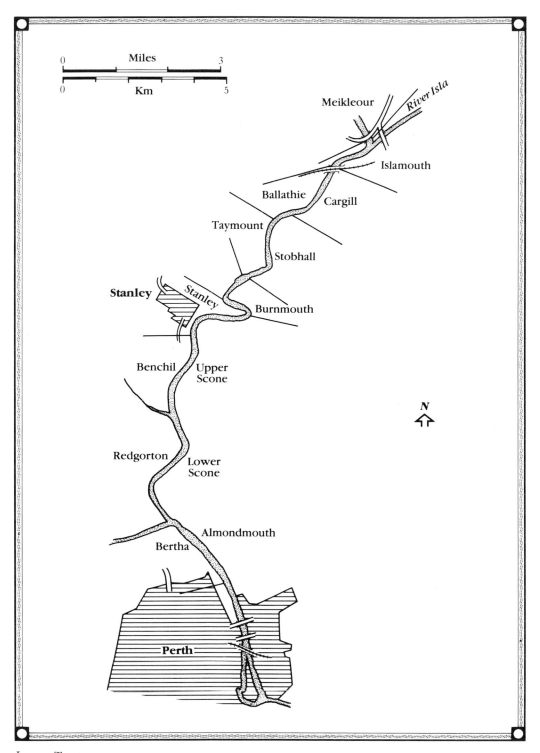

Lower Tay

similar thing can happen on the Spey. Remember, these rivers have truly vast catchment areas and there are times, yes even in Scotland, when rain can be fairly localised.

On the Tay system, the Isla that joins the main river at Islamouth is the only tributary to drain in from the east. Therefore, when the rain falls on the eastern coast Isla rises in flood, colouring the lower Tay, while the middle and upper river and their tributaries, all being fed from the west, remain clear. There is another factor besides this meteorological geography: the Isla has no loch of note, either natural or artificial. Contrast this to Loch Tay or Faskally, on Tay and Tummel respectively. Both of these act as sumps to filter rising coloured water, and in consequence the Tay is normally running clear. Indeed, only a few rivers such as the Aberdeenshire Dee can beat it in this respect. Let a dirty spate run off the Isla, however, and its effect on lower Tay fishing, while middle and upper beats continue to fish well, can be frustrating. This comparison of upper Tay and Tummel with the Isla clearly points to the underlying value of lochs to the headwaters of a river system and their effects on fishing on the river as a whole, in addition to storing a head of water in order to maintain flow. Natural, fresh water, as in the case of Loch Tay, is of far greater value than artificial stale water spates as seen in hydroised rivers.

The effect of the Isla on lower Tay, in just the same way as Tummel affected middle Tay, is to increase its flow still further. At Islamouth itself, and for a mile or more downstream of the junction, Tay runs quickly through a succession of rapids and pools. A friend of mine said that when he fished this stretch for the first time he could not help being reminded of the Spey, except that the Tay runs at twice its size. It is not until Ballathie is passed that the Tay begins to lose its added impetus, and then there are but three short miles to the Linn of Campsie. Linns are narrow rocky gorges that funnel the water into a white maelstrom before crashing into deep, rock-girt cauldron pools. The Linns of Campsie are similar to the Linns of Dee, upstream of Braemar, only on a very much larger scale.

One would expect the Linns of Campsie to act as a temperature pool, an obstruction to ascending fish until the water had warmed to above 42 degrees. That this is not entirely true is observed by the capture of salmon right up at Loch Tay, and spread all down the river, on the opening day of the season. What was a more serious obstruction to their passage, however, was the Stanley Weir. This lies less than a mile below the Linns and, in former times, held back many fish until the water temperature was above 40 degrees. Then it was breached with fish passes at three points, and the problem was very largely solved.

The Tay maintains its strong flow down to Redgorton, is subsequently joined by the Almond and very soon enters the tidal waters reaching right up to the City of Perth.

If one had to state which of the lower Tay beats produced the greatest sport, it would be a hard task to make a sensible answer. They are all, in their time, quite splendid. Junction pools are normally associated with outstanding salmon sport, and so Islamouth and Almondmouth must be included in the list. As already mentioned, it is certainly rumoured that Islamouth may well be the most prolific salmon pool in Scotland, with a catch running into four figures. And, in compiling a list of the greatest of lower Tay beats who could, in all seriousness, leave out Ballathie and Cargill just below Islamouth, or Taymount and Stobhall below them, then Stanley and Upper and Lower Scone, Benchil and Redgorton? All these are far famed names in the world of salmon fishing. But, of course, those who know the Tay well will be smiling at my list, for there is not one beat, from Islamouth down to the City of Perth, that has not been mentioned! Let me leave it at that.

Traditionally, it is the opening and closing months of the season, spring and autumn, which produce the best sport on the Tay. Tay became a river with an outstanding reputation for producing big springers with an average weight in excess of 15lb, but in recent seasons, extremely sad to say, the spring run has faded. Besides the sheer quantity of fish, the quality has also fallen – what salmon are caught in the opening months of the Tay season in recent years have had an average weight closer to 10lb. Scale reading will confirm that whereas the Tay formerly saw a majority of three-sea-winter salmon returning in spring, modern fish are of the two-sea-winter type.

And so it is that Tay beats and anglers have come to look to the late summer and autumn for the cream of their fishing in modern times. The runs at this time have been steadily increasing for the past thirty years. It should be noted, however, that this is not an autumn run in the truest sense as seen on Tweed and Nith, where the seasons are extended through to the end of November in order to make the most of the late harvest. On the Tay, the main runs are best considered as late summer, or early autumn at latest, with fishing at its best in August and September. By the close of the season on 15 October really fresh run fish are becoming fairly scarce, and most salmon in the Tay by then will be showing clearly that they are close to spawning. No true sportsman takes any pleasure in catching heavily pregnant females or cock fish sporting their tartan trews.

It is during this late summer fishing that the chance of catching one of the Tay monster salmon becomes a real possibility, and it is on this lower section of the river that chances are best. Look at the dates and places of a list of Tay salmon that exceeded 50lb in weight: Loch Tay produced two 50-pounders, one in 1874 and one in 1880; middle Tay, besides Georgina Ballantine's record salmon, has produced but two more, a 50- and a 52-pounder both from Kinnaird. Now look at the record of lower Tay beats.

Ballathie produced a 54-pounder in 1969 and a 51-pounder in October 1913, as well as a 51½-pounder on a sea trout fly in July 1875 for Mr J. Gellatly.

Cargill was the beat where Sir Stuart Coates Bt took a 53-pounder on a Jock Scott fly in October 1923.

Taymount's Findford Stream was the scene for Lord Ruthven's capture of a 54-pounder in 1884, and Findford Head produced a 50-pounder for Commander H. Clarke-Jerwoise on 23 September 1883, again to a Jock Scott.

At Stobhall, a Wilkinson fly produced a 55½-pounder in October 1903 and a

Black Dog fly was the downfall of a 53-pounder in October 1898. A 50-pounder was also taken at Stobhall in July 1928.

Stanley produced the earliest-season monster salmon – a 61-pounder caught in March 1870 by Mr J. Haggar on a minnow. The Marquis of Zetland, either before or after his lesson in switch casting from Alexander Grant, had a 55-pounder from the Mill Stream in October 1883 on a Claret Major fly.

Scone Palace produced a 55½-pounder from just below Woody Isle on 26 September 1898, taken on a minnow by Captain A. G. Goodwin. Lower Scone had its 53-pounder taken on fly by Mr P. M. Pritchard on 19 October 1924, before the closing date of the season was moved forward.

Almondmouth, lowest of the great Tay beats, produced a 54-pounder for Mr J. T. Ness in October 1942, as recorded in the book *Where to Fish*.

And finally, lest anybody reading this book on 'great salmon beats' should be foolish enough to disregard public waters, the Perth Association Water has produced the second largest recorded rod and line Tay salmon, a 61½-pounder taken on the worm by Mr T. Stewart in October 1907, as well as a 53-pounder for Mr Dow in 1915 and a 51-pounder for Mr Fletcher in October 1903 on a minnow.

Lists of such remarkable salmon and how, when and where they were caught have always made fascinating reading. I would dearly love to know how many of those salmon which fell for the fly were actually taken by casting it or, as happens so much on the Tay, by harling the fly behind a boat. Perhaps of lesser interest in these more conservationally minded days are records of sheer quantities of fish caught. However, two at least of the recorded Tay bags are most revealing, for they disclose not only quantity but also the quality of Tay salmon. At Lower Stanley on 9 March 1922, Major Baker Carr caught seventeen salmon. Together they weighed 276lb to give an average weight of 16lb, his best fish being a 30-pounder. Charles A. Murray, however, beat the Major's bag, both in terms of quantity and quality, with twenty fish weighing a total of 365lb to give an average weight of 18½lb. This bag was taken in autumn on the Taymount water. Quite incredible fishing and fish, all taken on fly.

Today, in terms of quantity alone, it may still be possible for such bags to be taken. However, it would be rather more than optimistic to hope that average weights would even approach the same class, half being more realistic.

No discussion of the lower Tay and its mighty salmon would be complete without mention of an encounter made by Dr Browne, Bishop of Bristol, on the last day but one of the season of 1868. It is fully described in A. E. Gathorne-Hardy's book *The Salmon*, published in 1898.

Bishop Browne was fishing that part of the Tay at the junction with the Earn, below Perth and actually in the estuary. Harling was the chosen method, employing minnows on a trio of rods.

High tide had been at about 10am. The Bishop and his party in the boat were

The Tay at Perth – mightiest of Scottish rivers

fishing the ebb, and hooked a salmon at 12.30pm. The big fish chose the minnow on the weakest of the three lines, a makeshift affair comprising two trout lines, on which the splice had not been tried, to give a total length of 120 yards.

From the very start, as the writer clearly describes, the fish was playing the boat and its occupants rather than the other way about. Three hours later, and many dramas behind them, the boat was approaching Newburgh, well down the Firth of Tay. Besides having to contend with the fish, the Bishop had a mutinous passenger who was so keen to get ashore and out of the wet, cold and hungry position in which he found himself that he threatened to jump overboard and swim for the shore. (If the passenger had been out with me, rather than a Bishop, he might have been given a helping hand to send him on his way!)

By now the tide had changed and was on the flow. At first, this put the fish into a rare panic, causing it to dash back up towards the river. And it was then that he leapt clean out of the water. Up until now, they had guessed the salmon to be foul hooked, as explanation for his tremendous fighting strength. But now the hook was seen, fairly in the mouth of 'a monster as large as a well grown boy'.

It was then that one strand of the line which had suffered such strain parted. The boatman raced after the fish, and the Bishop was able to reel up line until the parted strand was back on the reel. From that point on, the exertions of the boatman knew no bounds as he fought to keep close to the salmon and prevent the frayed section running out from the reel. It was 6.30pm. The Bishop and his boatman had been playing and being played by the salmon for six hours.

By this time, following the fish upriver, they had returned to their original position at the pier from which they had cast off seven hours earlier. After much pleading with folk on the shore, a second boat was launched to pick up the complaining passenger who was sent away with a plea to return with food and light. An hour passed before the second boat returned with a lantern, two candles, cakes and cheese 'enough for a week' and, thoughtful folk, a bottle of whisky.

The good Bishop now hit upon a masterly plan, inspired by prayer or dram we cannot tell. A spare rod with a stout salmon line was got ready. During a lull in the salmon's proceedings, a good knot was tied between the new line and the old line still holding the salmon, and the old line snapped above the knot. The problem now, of course, was that the knot would not pass through the rod rings. From having to keep right up to the fish, the boatman now had to maintain a respectful distance.

The tide turned again. The fish had now been hooked for ten hours. It was decided that they would follow the fish until dawn, when the Bishop should be set ashore to make a final stand. But the fish was not for waiting, and, as he had when the tide changed before, went into a frenzy of activity.

The Bishop withstood a good half hour of the salmon's incessant fury. Then they could plainly hear the mighty salmon thrashing on the surface, a sure sign that he was finished and the end of the mighty battle close at hand. Now they had him.

It was then, when final triumph seemed so close, that the salmon rushed at the boat. The Bishop reeled in fast and hard on a slack line. He reeled on, but there was no sign of resistance. Up popped the minnow, minus the hooks. No words could describe their feelings at that time. Jimmy, the boatman, rowed back to the pier in total silence.

There is a sequel to the story, as told by A. Courtney Williams in his book *Angling Diversions*, published in 1945. He describes a salmon, a 71-pounder, which was displayed at Messrs Grove's shop in Westminster during 1871. It had a length of 52in and a girth of 31in. Courtney Williams stated:

> It might well have been the record British rod-caught salmon, as it was hooked at noon one day in the Tay by the Bishop of Bristol (Bishop Browne), who played it for 10½ hours when the trace broke. Two days later it was taken in the nets, with the Bishop's small phantom still in its jaws.

Believe that or not as you choose. Personally, I believe that there are far too many inconsistencies. For one thing, writing but thirty years after the event, Gathorne-Hardy gives the year as 1868 while, in the account of the sequel, it is given as 1871. And, one would think, if this fish was the one displayed in Westminster then surely Gathorne-Hardy would have heard of and mentioned it? Equally, Courtney Williams describes the small phantom being found in the salmon's jaw, but the earlier account states that the minnow came back, minus its hooks. And, although I have been unable to ascertain the closed season dates of the time, would the nets have been operating after the close of the rod and line season? No, I am sorry, but in my mind the two tales do not tally and it is the first, rather than the last, which I accept. Or was another mighty Tay salmon hooked and lost at a later date?

That, of course, leaves us guessing at the true size of 'a monster as large as a well grown boy'. Could it perhaps have been brother or sister to the Tay 84-pounder taken by Wullie Walker in a sparling net? We shall never know.

TAY FISHING

Many aspects of Tay fishing have been touched upon in this chapter. Nevertheless, it will do no harm to draw them all together into this brief, summarising section, for here we have some of the greatest salmon beats and fishing in the British Isles and the world. If there be but one minor criticism of the Tay, it is that it does not lend itself well, due simply to the enormity and scale of its pools, to fishing the fly. In fact, fly fishing on the Tay tends very largely to be restricted, in the eyes of most anglers, to those times when the mighty river falls to reveal what are, in effect, rivers within the river. This is no exaggeration. One mighty headstream leading into a Tay pool may, in times of low water, be split into two or three streams that would be respected in their own right on a river of lesser scale.

That the Tay spring fishings are suffering a period of decline cannot be refuted. There are weeks now available for let during the spring on some beats which, up until recent times, would have been jealously guarded by the tenant until increasing frailty or death moved him on to make way for another man who, very probably, would have been taking a let at some less fortunate time for many years and waiting his chance of a prime week. The thought of letting spring rods on a daily basis, as occurs on some Tay beats today would, in the past, have been unheard of. Spring salmon still run the Tay, however, and are caught.

Spring fishing is now normally best in the lower Tay. Salmon certainly will run the Stanley Weir now that it has been breached. Prior to this access being opened up, catches of twenty springers in a day from Catholes on Stanley were made. And salmon will run the Campsie Linn. But even so, even if the combination of Weir and Linn is not insurmountable, they do still hold back a significant proportion of early season fish. Those fish that ascend the Linn will, after their exertions, spend time in Taymount and Stobhall. Put these factors together and it can fairly be said that the best of what is admittedly diminished spring fishing will take place between Islamouth and Almondmouth.

Fish are certainly taken on upper beats and on the Tummel at the start of the season. However, these bear some close consideration. Among those salmon taken on the Tay in October, there will be a number of silvery fresh specimens which are widely accepted as harbingers of the spring run. Remembering that it is said that Tay salmon enter the river on every week of each month of the season, other early running spring fish will enter the Tay over the following months. Some of these early fish make their way right up to Loch Tay where they overwinter, and some of them are caught at the start of the season. In January and February, however, the Scottish winter is more severe and while some salmon will run on to upstream beats and the loch, others will tarry on lower beats until such time as warmer water sets them on the move.

Early season Tay fishing, be it on a lower river beat or right up at Loch Tay, relies heavily on hovering a spinner, spoon, plug or fly behind a boat. On the loch it is known as trolling. On the river it is called harling. In either case, most fishermen's opinions of it is that it is a cold and boring method of fishing, and relies almost entirely on the skills of the boatman rather than the angler. But then a salmon takes the lure – it may be a big yellow and black tube fly or a Rapala, Kynoch Killer, Lucky Louie or Tay Lure – and as the multiplier screeches and the rod bends to the first searing run of what may be a 20- or 30-pounder, all thoughts of cold and discomfort disappear.

May is traditionally recognised as marking an end to spring fishing on the lower beats. Boats are taken off for any running repairs that may be required before sport picks up in late summer. Whether or not this tradition will be maintained now hangs in the balance – the point is that by June, given rain and decent water levels, lower beats at least can expect sport with summer salmon and grilse. However, what has been happening right up to the present time, which has invalidated attempts to fish seriously with rod and line, has been the netting activities. It is estimated that during dry summers a combination of sweep nets on Scone Estate and below Perth can account for up to 96 per cent of these summer runs, only four out of a hundred salmon escaping the deadly meshes.

Surely, if these nets were taken off, phenomenal sport for rod and line interests would ensue? After all, the stocks entering the river would increase by some *twenty-five* times. However, stopping nets or even attempting to control them on a river like the Tay is a highly complicated business. Let me just describe the situation as existing towards the end of the '88 season.

The Atlantic Salmon Conservation Trust, in an attempt to buy off nets on the Tay, has joined forces with the Tay Foundation. Approaches to Tay Salmon Fisheries have revealed that they are prepared to sell. The district council have agreed to discuss selling. In both cases, the sellers are talking about conditions.

The main condition is that nobody else, upstream of their netting stations, should carry on netting. There is but one netting proprietor upstream of their own positions: these are the Trustees of Viscount Stormont, who have been bought off for a limited period of five years for a sum of £8,500 per annum, by the Tay District Salmon Fisheries Board. The District Council, for its part, has at least agreed not to grant a 15-year extension to its existing lease with Insch Fishings.

This is all very well. It certainly seems that the commitment is there to curtail Tay salmon netting. In addition, the weekend slap, the period when nets may not operate, has been increased by a further sixteen hours. What is actually happening, however, is that at least one Tay netting company, to make up for the increased slap period, has increased its netsmen's shifts from eight to ten hours. Also, several netting stations are operating a shared-crop scheme for their crews – the more they catch, the more they earn. These share-croppers are filling in vacancies at netting stations that have not been operated for years.

The upshot is that, at one level and in one area, we see serious moves to limit Tay netting and increase salmon stocks in the river. At another, we see equally strong efforts to ensure that what some netsmen are giving up shall be taken by other netsmen – gaining on the swings what they lose on the roundabouts. Personally, I am not prepared to make any sort of prediction as to what the likely outcome, in terms of rod and line fishing and salmon escapement, is likely to be. But we can all hope, at least, that things are about to get better in terms of Tay spring and early summer fishing.

What does put an end to netting, at least of the legal variety, is the close of their season on 20 August. After that, Tay beats will start to fill with the late summer runs, leading into early autumn. This autumn run will be in full swing by mid-September. Water levels play a most important part, as always, and levels must be maintained to bring in more and more salmon with each succeeding tide and create a steady upstream movement in the fish. These salmon will mostly weigh in the teens of pounds, with plenty of 20-, some 30- and a few 40-pounders among them. Among the tail enders of this early autumn run will be the earliest of the spring fish – salmon that will spend practically an entire year in the river before spawning. And now the cycle of returning Tay salmon has turned full circle.

CHAPTER 13

TWEED

What sort of salmon river is Tweed? It could be fairly argued that it has potential to be the greatest of them all. Perhaps these are merely the prejudiced thoughts of a Scottish Borderer. If so, they may be excused for Tweed has that effect upon us. Read, for example, what Thomas 'Tod' Stoddart had to say on the subject:

> Let ither anglers chuse their ain,
>   An ither waters tak the lead;
> O' Hielan streams we covet nane,
>   But gie to us the Bonnie Tweed!
> And gie to us the cheerfu' burn
>   That steels into its valley fair –
> The streamlets that at ilka turn
>   Sae softly meet and mingle there –
>
> The lonesome Talla and the Lyne,
>   And Manor wi' its mountain rills,
> An' Ettrick whose waters twine
>   Wi' Yarrow frae the forest hills;
> An' Gala, too, an' Teviot bright,
>   An' many a stream o' playfu' speed;
> Their kindred valleys a' unite
>   Among the braes o' bonnie Tweed.
>
> Oh the Tweed! the bonnie Tweed!
>   O' rivers it is the best;
> Angle here or angle there,
>   Troots are soomin' ilka where,
> Angle east or west.

Tweed is as fascinating as it is marvellous. For one thing, you will perhaps have noted that I write Tweed rather than 'the' Tweed. This writing convention seems to be lost in the mists of Scottish literal history, and is far from being universally recognised. For example, Scrope did not stand by it and neither, come to that, do those of my family who have lived on its banks for generations. And so, if anybody has a definitive answer on the subject of 'To the, or not to the,' perhaps they would be caring enough to write and let me know which it should be!

To a Border Scot or Northumbrian, Tweed is more than a river. It flows through the history of these lands, through a bloody time of the war of two nations, the

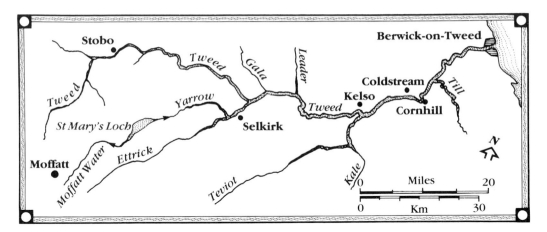

Tweed and its tributaries

struggle for independence, and through centuries of raiding and rieving. Lest the scale of the suffering involved be underestimated, it is said that, following the visit of one English king, Tweed ran red with blood for three weeks. Neither side could claim to be not guilty of horrendous deeds. Scots historians talk proudly of the outcome of the Battle of Bannockburn, but draw a veil over the wicked fate of those English troops who attempted to surrender. Neither do they describe the activities of the Scottish solidery who, following the battle, set off on the rampage through the northern counties of England. But these deeds are long past and, on the whole, forgotten. Today, local rivalries are settled with blood curdling war cries only on the rugby pitches that proliferate in each and every Border town.

And yet, it is perhaps an old sense of animosity that has created problems in managing the river system as a salmon fishery. Below Gainslaw, from where it is but 4½ miles to the sea, the river is entirely in England. Moving upstream from Gainslaw, the next 15 miles find the southern bank in England and the northern bank in Scotland. Above that, the river lies entirely in Scotland. With the knowledge that, historically, it is the English bank and mouth of Tweed which was always netted, and that while drift netting at sea is permitted off Northumberland it is illegal off the Scottish coast, it is easy to see that middle and upper Tweed Scottish proprietors have been tearing their hair out at the activities of their English neighbours. In recent times, netting pressure has been eased, but it still remains to see what long-term improvements will be brought about. Indeed, we are now faced with the prospect of what were once netting stations being put over to rod and line fishing.

Because of this system of 'dual nationality', the river has been treated separately since 1771 when the first specific legislation applying solely to Tweed was introduced. An independent board of 'Tweed Commissioners' was formed in 1859 to manage the river, with far greater powers than a District Board.

Looking at the river's history, both ancient and recent, it is almost a surprise to the uninitiated to discover that Tweed is rated among the four classic, great salmon rivers of Scotland: Dee, Spey, Tay and Tweed. Salmon stocks returning to the river have been raped for centuries, by both legal and illegal nets. Tweed lent its name to the woven material produced in the large number of mills situated on its banks. Mills in themselves have created pollution, at one time uncontrolled, and have attracted the growth of a host of Border towns, creating still more pollution. Water is abstracted from the headwaters in order to supply Edinburgh.

Tweed survives all this but, knowing it, while we can be happy for its standing, we should also see it as a shadow of what it once was and, far more important, of what it might be again. One wonders what it is that has sustained Tweed salmon and fishing throughout its long history. Perhaps the most significant feature is the vast extent of its breeding and nursery areas. It is, after all, second only to the Tay in length for a Scottish river. And then it is served by a great network of tributaries, a number of which are virtually salmon rivers in their own right. In Tweed's lower reaches, it is joined by the Till. Higher up, a fisherman's eye turns to tributaries such as Ettrick, Jed, Teviot and Yarrow. Tweed may be second to the Tay in terms of the length and size of the parent river but, put together with its tributaries, it must surely be out in front in the race to provide spawning grounds.

At the present time, Tweed is recognised as the autumn river, without peer. Solway rivers have their back-end runs, it is true, but they cannot come close to matching the sheer quantity of late salmon and sport seen on the eastern river. Note that autumn fishing in the Borders, from September through until the end of November, is not the pursuit of dull, coloured fish that entered the river in spring and summer. Tweed enjoys runs of sea-fresh fish through and beyond the tail of the season. In terms of fly fishing alone, this makes Tweed significant because the rule after 14 September, traditionally when netting stops, is 'fly-only'.

The spring run of Tweed salmon, on the other hand, has been in a sad state of decline for many years. This is not to say that Tweed spring salmon fishing no longer exists. Of course not, and beats below Kelso can still have their moments of early season glory, but they are as nothing to the old days.

There is statistical information to show that the nature of Tweed salmon runs has been cyclical, with the main runs swinging from spring to autumn on a thirty-year cycle, and then back again. All that can be said, however, is that the time for a reversion to primarily spring runs came and went a few seasons ago. There can surely be little doubt that outside forces are responsible. Common suggestions are the level of high seas netting, at a truly horrendous level of efficiency. And yet, why is it that the Dee maintains its spring runs when all about are losing theirs? On this, there are plenty of suggestions, but no definitive answers. One theory that has been much publicised is the notion of 'over-cutting of redds'. This suggests that early season salmon spawn first, then later running fish come to the redds, lay their own eggs, and, in the process, the eggs of the earlier fish are swept away and destroyed. It sounds plausible, at one level, but when it is considered in greater depth, the fertilised salmon egg is very tough and, anyway, if it were true, why were spring fish not wiped out many centuries ago? Remember the cyclical nature of Tweed runs, and then

Part of the autumn harvest on Tweedside

explain why the spring salmon were ever able to return to a dominant position not once but time after time. And, at another level, the 'over-cutting of redds' idea can be seen as nothing more than an attempt to offer a case for the netsmen when they seek to increase their annual catch by taking more autumn fish, and saying that they are doing it for the benefit of re-establishing the spring runs. No; we would be foolish to fall for that one, on Tweed or anywhere else.

Anybody who is interested in Tweed and its history must make a point of reading William Scrope's book, *Days and Nights of Salmon Fishing in the Tweed and Other Rivers*, to give it its full and rather ponderous title. First published in 1843, it gives an illuminated insight into salmon and the ways of the fisherman during the early half of last century. Incidentally, for those who may wonder at the inclusion of 'nights' of fishing in the title, the practice of leistering was still legal at that time. At night, sportsmen were happy to join the locals, laying aside their fishing rods in favour of a leister. These leisters were fishing spears, traditionally having five barbed prongs. The normal plan was to set out in boats and 'burn the water' – bright blazing torches being used to see as well as stupefy the resting salmon, which were then speared. Sir Walter Scott, the great Scottish writer, was keen on this form of amusement. Of course, this was done in the days before monofilament nets and high seas netting reduced salmon stocks, and pressure from sporting gentlemen for rod and line fishing was still relatively small. Scrope's account of his fishing experiences over a quarter century, starting in 1820, makes absolutely fascinating and superbly entertaining reading, the man's wit and ability to tell a tale shining out of each and every page. I have often thought that it would be no bad idea for a monument to be erected to the memory of Scrope, to be placed where the great man's spirit can view his beloved river.

Having talked of the cyclical nature of Tweed salmon runs, it is fascinating to discover from Scrope's book that, in his time, salmon ran the river virtually throughout the season, although, even then, the best of the sport was undoubtedly enjoyed in the back-end. This state of affairs continued from Scrope's time right through to the start of this century, with the best sport for the rod coming in the latter half of September and then October and November. This comes as little surprise, considering netting ceased on 15 September!

But that, surely, is enough of the past. What is the state of fish and fishing on Tweed today? To look at the situation in more detail, it is clear that, while the autumn may see the heaviest runs, there are still substantial numbers of both early spring and summer salmon. February 1 is opening day on the Tweed and salmon will be caught, although it is rare, and a mild winter phenomenon, for any to have ventured above the Cauld at Kelso, a 'cauld' being alternatively known as a weir. So long as Tweed stays at a good running height, salmon numbers continue to build up until May, when rainfall diminishes, the river level falls and, traditionally, the nets have a field day.

In mentioning nets and the nature of spring salmon, I recall a conversation I had on the banks of the Tweed above Berwick some years ago. You know, there was a time in the fish-rich days of the sixties when it seemed that rods and nets might be able to co-exist. It was a period when there were so many fish in our rivers that there seemed to be plenty for everybody. Anyway, a rodsman would still talk to a netsman, and we were asking an old hand at a netting station about a fairly red fish that he was carrying up to the fish locker. He explained that this was a type of salmon that the netsmen know as Westerners. These salmon come into the river with the rest of the spring fish but, for some reason known only to themselves, change their minds and decide that they have come too early. They fall back to the sea, presumably to return at a later date so long, that is, as they do not end up in a net! Salmon are certainly complex creatures. I asked the netsman why they called them Westerners. He was not sure. In regard to the effect of limitation or cessation of netting activity on Tweed and other rivers – a relatively new and very welcome reversal in salmon fortunes – it is still early days to be talking about definite trends emerging. With more fish given access to the rivers and their beats, however, there can be little if any doubt that things for the rod and line fisherman are bound to improve.

Spring fish from Tweed are noticeably small in stature. Experienced fishermen expect fish of an average weight of about 8lb, and a 20-pounder really is a rarity. You must go back 70 years to find a Tweed springer of more than 40lb – a salmon caught at Rutherford. It has been questioned whether this might not have indeed been a very late running autumn fish. It is possible.

Salmon that return to Tweed in summer are, unexpectedly, larger than the spring fish. Equally, grilse come with them, and these game little fish are often far smaller, of weights that we normally associate with sea trout. Not Tweed sea trout, you understand, certainly not the big sea trout of Tweed that run with the autumn salmon, which are caught on heavy salmon tackle and can weigh over 20lb, as did the Tweed fish in recent seasons which set the new British record. The fish I am talking about are pretty little silver bars, weighing from a couple to a few pounds. With these smaller grilse, larger salmon, and all weights in between, the summer stock in Tweed could have a rosy future.

Then comes autumn, nets are nothing but a memory and, as water levels rise, Tweed sport really comes into its own with the equinoctial rains. Salmon come pouring into the beats in their thousands, and they are fresh, clean and silvery fish. They run fast for the upper river, as hard as any fish, with the spawning drive forcing them on. It is only in times of low water that these autumn fish are likely to get held up in the lower beats although the best of the autumn fishing is almost invariably above Kelso.

Something has already been said about the weight of spring and summer salmon. Looking at the autumn run, it is perhaps unfortunate that what Tweed has gained in quantity, it may have lost in average weight. Tweed salmon of the autumn months used to average about 16lb or more. Nowadays, the increasing number of smaller fish of about 8lb has pulled that average down to nearer 10lb, maybe slightly more. The bigger fish are still there, however. Twenty and 30-pounders are still fairly common, and once in a while a 40-pounder will be grassed, so perhaps we should not complain too much. Given the choice, I for one would have two smaller fish and one large one rather than two biggies alone.

It must be noted that Tweedsiders are not prepared to accept Georgina Ballantyne's Tay salmon as the true record salmon. That honour they claim for Lord Home's salmon of 69lb, taken in the year 1743. There is absolutely no doubt that this leviathan fish existed or, indeed, any argument as to the fact that it was accurately weighed. Nor is the fact that the eighth Earl of Home was fishing with a rod of 22ft and a horse-hair line. What is in dispute, however, is just how many ounces there were to the pound at that date, and so the salmon and Lord Home of long ago have to bow out to Miss Ballantyne's fish.

Another Tweed salmon came close to being a record breaker. It was hooked during an autumn afternoon's fishing on Bermersyde. The scrap continued between fisherman and fish until well after dark. The fish won when it finally snapped the gut cast. Next morning, it was discovered that, following the epic struggle, poachers had visited the beat. Whether it was that they were unable to carry away the mighty fish in one piece, or whether to show the angler what might have been, they left the tail piece. It alone weighed 35lb.

The Homes seem to have been able to charm big Tweed salmon into giving themselves up. That probable record has been discussed. Later in the same century, William, Earl of Home had a salmon of 61lb. And then there was General Home's 51½lb fish, caught on a Jock Scott at Birgham Dub in 1902.

Other outstanding Tweed salmon, all taken in the autumn, include Mr Pryor's fish of 57½lb, taken on a Silver Wilkinson at Upper Floors in October 1886; Mr Brereton's 55-pounder, again on a Wilkinson, from Mertoun in 1889; a salmon of the same weight taken by W. A. Kidson; Dr Fison's Norham fish of 51½lb in 1922; Howard St George's 51-pounder, caught on a Jock Scott in 1921, and a salmon of 50½lb caught at Birgham Dub in 1925 by Mr Rudd. Incidentally, although the pattern is not known in every case, it should perhaps be pointed out that all these salmon, being caught after the nets had ceased operations, would have been taken on the fly.

Besides reducing size, there is one other question mark hanging over the whole business of autumn fishing. It seems inevitable that fish of the spring and summer runs, now stale, coloured and on the verge of spawning, will be killed along with the fresh, autumn runners. Some fishermen, sadly, cannot bring themselves to return any fish that they catch. It is saddening to witness their attempts to justify taking a salmon that has already donned its tartan drawers. 'It will do for smoking' is but a lame excuse, and no sort of an explanation. Besides anything else, you can't make a silk purse out of a sow's ear and, the cost of smoking being what it is, it only makes sense to reserve the best and freshest fish for this process. On the other hand, it has to be accepted that a significant proportion of those fish that we try to release alive will not survive the experience, particularly if they have engulfed one of the modern generation of articulated flies necessitating the removal of the treble hook from the fish's vomer.

Finding a solution is not easy. To stop Tweed's salmon season earlier would surely be a negative, protectionist approach rather than the positive line of management for conservation. At one level, it certainly might help that the bulk of the river's spring and summer run should have moved up into the upper river and its tributaries. Thus, the problem is virtually removed from middle and lower Tweed beats. There is still, however, an awful lot of fishing on the upper river. Again, the protectionist road seems fraught with problems and I, for one, if I fished the Upper Tweed on a regular basis would not stand for curtailing my season when the fatter, lower beats were enjoying an already far longer season. One could wish that more upper river and tributary fishermen would perhaps set aside their articulated flies and treble hooks after the start of October, and resort to the big singles of grandfather's day. It is far easier to remove such a hook from a gravid fish that is to be returned than extracting a treble with all three points embedded back close to the gills. Of course, it is one thing to suggest these voluntary controls, but quite another to achieve an adoption of them by the majority. However, having banned bait from the river on the grounds that it is unsporting, perhaps this is a matter to which the authorities might like to turn their attention. Dare one go so far as to suggest a £50 fine for having a gravid cock fish in your possession, and a £100 fine for a heavily pregnant

Playing a Tweed autumn salmon

hen? Would these fines be sufficient to deter those taking the hens to sell for their spawn to poachers?

Further on this point, leading from what may be questionable tackle to that which is downright illegal, there is that despicable object, the Walkerburn Angel. This is a heavily weighted treble that makes little pretence as to its true purpose – to rip into the flank or back of a resting salmon. There is very little that is better in brass tubes, with further weight added in the form of lead underwrapping, or head, or a pierced bullet slipped onto the trace, the addition of large sea swivels onto the trace, or any other contraption that is so obviously intended to rake the big treble with which the fly is armed across the backs of salmon. It is an absolute disgrace that this sort of tackle, and lead-cored lines are included in this condemnation, are still allowed on a river where they choose to ban bait on the grounds that prawn and shrimp are unsporting. Sniggling, snatching, raking or call it what you will may be most openly publicised and condemned on the public waters in the Peebles area, but that is only because there are numerous witnesses to the event. Do not imagine that such things do not happen on private beats. People who will take a salmon in this way should really be chased back under the stone from which they crawled out. This sort of thing is an insult to such a fine river. Also, it is quite enough time and words to be spent on describing the activities of what, fortunately, are a small minority. Let us leave it at that, and take a look at the various sections of the river and their beats.

UPPER TWEED AND TRIBUTARIES

Upper Tweed is generally recognised as being that section from the source downstream as far as Ettrick Mouth, between Selkirk and Melrose. Its source is known as the Wells of Tweed, and is away in the west, on the border between Dumfriesshire and Lanarkshire. Indeed, there is a rhyme to the effect that 'Tweed and Clyde both rise on the same hillside,' and this one small hill on the watershed with Clyde flowing to the west and Tweed to the east can lay another claim to fame because, just a short distance away, the source is found for the Annan, among the most prolific salmon rivers of the Solway.

It was said earlier that from its source, at a height of 1500ft, Tweed runs in an easterly direction. That is not quite true. For the first six miles of its existence, the little burn that is to become one of Scotland's mightiest rivers is heading practically due north. Then it begins to turn slightly more to the east where it meets up with the outflows from Fruid and then Talla reservoirs. It is notable that the headwaters of Tweed are found on much lower ground than, say, the Dee or Spey. And, in just the same way that one finds the most productive agricultural ground the closer one gets to sea level, so this river's comparatively low-lying breeding and nursery grounds must surely be an advantage to its productivity.

After being joined by the reservoir outflows, the infant Tweed flows another six miles to its junction with the Biggar Water at the village of Broughton, before taking an eastward turn and running for the sea.

In the run from Tweed Well to Broughton, the river falls 900ft. It is clear therefore that from this point onward, the river becomes a majestic lowland flow of deep dubs and haughs.

Before Peebles, it is joined by two more tributaries. Manor Water flows in from the south, and Lyne Water from the north. From Peebles, being joined by a number of minor tributaries along the way, Tweed passes Innerleithen and flows on through the village of Walkerburn. Six miles below Walkerburn, close to the Border town of Selkirk, it is joined by one of its principal tributaries, the Ettrick. In fact, the Ettrick has already been joined by the Yarrow, flowing out of St Mary's Loch. 'The Dowie Dens o' Yarrow,' described by Sir Walter Scott, and the Ettrick can both provide good salmon sport in their season.

Taking the confluence with the Ettrick as the demarcation between upper and middle Tweed, what beats have been passed along the way? Moving downstream from Broughton, and leaving out the Peebles Burgh Water, they are Drumelzier, Stobo and Dawick Mill, Lyne, Haystoun, Horsburgh Castle, Nether Horsburgh and Kailzie, Cardrona, Traquair, Pirn, Caberstoun, Holylee, Elibank, Thornilee, Ashiesteel, Peel, Caddonlee, Caddonfoot, Yair, Fairnilee, Boldside and Sunderland Water, both upstream from Galashiels.

Boldide, or Boleside as it is alternatively spelt, actually lies downstream of the confluence of the Ettrick with Tweed and, for that reason, it can reasonably be argued that it is the uppermost of middle Tweed beats rather than the lowermost of upper Tweed. Be that as it may, it is an attractive water, and can be very productive in its time. W. B. 'Bill' Currie is among the foremost of Scottish salmon fishermen, and has vast experience of Scottish fishing. In his book, *Days and Nights of Game Fishing*, he devotes a chapter to describing a Big Day at Boleside. The time was the first week in October, significantly after netting on the lower river had stopped. Thursday found the river flowing at 2ft 7in on the gauge and, as Bill put it, 'just reeking of fish'. By the time that they stopped for an early lunch, he had five salmon and had lost one. Four other rods were fishing, and their catches brought the total to thirteen.

In the afternoon, when Bill's total reached eight, he decided to come ashore and let his son fish his rod. Bill, in the meantime, set off into Galashiels to buy the champagne. Reading that passage amused me greatly. Perhaps Bill will forgive me for sharing the reason. Bill appreciates the finer things in life, be it a great day's fishing, an operatic tenor, or a fine claret. I still recall the scene that a reporter from the *Liverpool Echo* stumbled upon one early spring in Galloway. Flurries of snow were being blown horizontally over the stone dyke behind which Bill and I were sheltering. With tweed caps pulled low over our eyes and Barbour jackets fastened tight to our chins, we were each sitting with a gin and tonic and slice of lemon, bickering about who should have remembered to bring ice. I never saw what that young lady wrote about her fishing trip to Galloway. Perhaps that is for the best. But I am digressing.

When Bill returned, his son was playing out a magnificent fish of 18½lb. Then

Bill started to fish again, trying the pool just one up from Abbotsford, home of Sir Walter Scott, and which he quite literally worked himself to death to pay for – that and settling the debts of a failed publishing enterprise. Bill caught another splendid fish of 17lb.

At the end of the day, Bill's rod had taken eleven salmon and, despite urgings from the keeper to try for the twelfth and thirteenth, to equal the Boleside record, it now seemed an irrelevance. The total between the five rods was twenty-six salmon. They drank their champagne. Certainly there have been greater days on middle and lower beats, but such a champagne-day reflects the quality throughout so much of Tweed's length that it cannot be ignored.

MIDDLE TWEED

The middle section of Tweed is recognised as the stretch below Ettrick Mouth down as far as Teviot's confluence. The Teviot is another major tributary, on the scale of the Ettrick, flowing down from the long valley above Hawick. In between Ettrick and Teviot, other notable tributaries are the Gala Water and Leader. Between these two tributaries stands the town of Melrose, a great centre for middle Tweed salmon fishing. This country is soaked in history. The heart of King Robert the Bruce was buried at Melrose Abbey. A few miles further downstream, at St Boswells, is Dryburgh Abbey, last resting-place of Sir Walter Scott and Field-Marshal Earl Haig. This history, certainly of older times, is intertwined with the stuff of myth, legend and folklore. Michael Scott, the legendary wizard of the Eildon Hills, was mentioned in Chapter 4 dealing with early flies as used by Scrope and his contemporaries on Tweedside – the Michael Scott, a wizard of a salmon fly. (Witches were believed in to the extent that when one was found, she was promptly burned at the stake. James I and VI was a great witch-finder, and instigator of many a ghastly barbecue in the Border hills! Thank goodness those days and nights are long past).

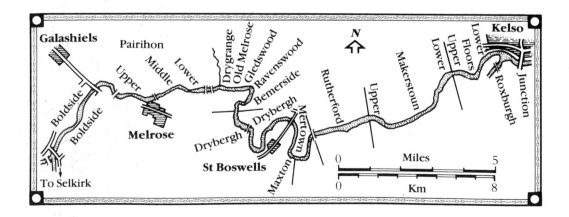

Middle Tweed

A young angler with his first salmon, an 18½-pounder from Boleside

far behind. From here on, Tweed flows through a magnificently rich, arable valley. The river down to Kelso has a succession of deep pools, streams, rapids and flats, as anybody who has driven the southerly bank, from Kelso past the old site of Roxburgh Castle, looking down on to Floors, will testify. Floors is the bottom-most of middle Tweed beats. Below Kelso cauld, the river is joined by the Teviot flowing into the famous Junction Pool where a man can pay the price of a small saloon car for his week's fishing.

Beats on this middle section of Tweed are far-famed names in the world of salmon fishing. Boleside has already been mentioned as either the lowest of upper beats or the highest on the middle. It is followed by the Pavilion Water, Upper Lower and Middle, then Dry Grange, Old Melrose, Gledswood, Ravenswood, Bemerside, Drybergh, Maxton, Mertoun, Rutherford, Makerstoun Upper and Lower, and finally Upper and Lower Floors. These beats undoubtedly comprise the very best section of Tweed. They provide excellent sport with both spring and autumn salmon, most notably the autumn, of course, in this age of diminished runs of springers. Looking at that list, I note that I have failed to mention the Tweedswood beat, not as famed as some of its neighbours, but an excellent stretch of salmon water nevertheless. If pressed, which would one say was the very best of these middle Tweed beats? Some would undoubtedly argue the case for Upper Floors, while others would champion the name of Mertoun. Just don't expect me to act as referee.

LOWER TWEED

The lower Tweed can be fairly taken as from Teviot Mouth and Junction Pool, below Kelso cauld, down to the sea. Having been joined by the Teviot, it is inevitable that

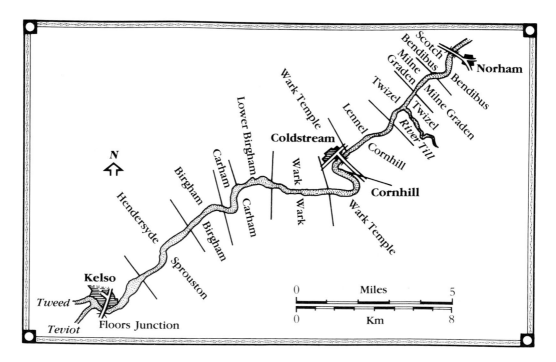

Lower Tweed

Tweed is a much bigger river below Kelso. It is equally inevitable that, despite flows being maintained down to Kelso, there has to come a point where the river loses its impetus. The fall from source to sea has simply begun to run out and, for much of its lower section, Tweed flows across a broad sweep of coastal plain.

Seven miles below Kelso, at Carham, the southern bank of the river passes into England. Whatever disputes there may be on other matters, at least the Scottish side, whiling away their Sunday closed time, do not have the prospect of rods fishing away on the opposite bank, as happens on the Border Esk. Separate legislation, pertaining solely to Tweed, ensures that, in this one small part of England, those in pursuit of migratory fish must observe the Sabbath.

It is in England that Tweed is joined by Till, at Tillmouth. This tributary, draining the slopes of the Cheviot Hills, home of the world-famous sheep breed, can produce good fishing with both salmon and sea trout. It is a deceptively calm and gentle river, but a trap for the unwary. Few rivers have claimed so many lives as to prompt a man to write about them. The identity of the author of the following rhyme is lost in the mists of antiquity, but his words are every bit as true today.

Says Tweed to Till
'What gars ye rin sae still?'
Says Till to Tweed
'Although ye rin wi' speed,
And I rin slaw,
for ae man that ye droon
I droon twa!'

The first man I heard that rhyme from was the late Tom Swan. The Swans are a particularly noted fishing family from Twizell at Tillmouth, although this particular Tom, despite being an exceptionally skilled angler, left his Tweedside home to farm in Kenya. After independence, he returned to his home country and, eventually, according to his last wish, his ashes were spread on to the river that he had loved so much throughout his boyhood and youth. Tom was a great character. He had fished each and every beat with rod and line from Melrose down as far as the netting stations, either with or without permission, for he was a bit of a rascal in that way. Only one beat had eluded him, and that was the Junction Pool of Tweed and Teviot. Then came the time that he and his wife had an hotel and one of the guests, booked to fish the Junction, was unable to arrive and asked Tom to fish his rod.

One sunny day, I actually got him to admit that he had once caught more than thirty Tweed salmon on fly in a day. He absolutely refused to say what his best bag had been, except that it had been taken on shrimp. Tom fished for the love and the sport of the thing and showed such a lack of interest in the salmon that he caught that there were times when his wife had to fetch and carry salmon that he had forgotten to bring home.

The Junction Pool, which can be treated as a great beat in its own right, is perhaps this country's, if not the world's, most famous salmon pool. Rents paid to fish this pool, particularly in October and November, are quite staggering but, then again, so is the potential salmon catch.

Below the Junction are a succession of fine salmon beats, the best of which include names like Hendersyde, Sprouston, Birgham and Carham. Mind you, these beats were more noted in the days of great spring fishing on Tweed. Early running salmon were in no hurry to pass up the lower river but nowadays, when autumn fishing is the thing on Tweed, most of the late running fish are travelling fast and hard, and it is the middle river that really scores. The higher the water level then, generally, the faster and higher up the salmon will travel.

Drawing a salmon to the gillie's waiting net below the Junction Pool and bridge at Kelso

CHAPTER 14

ENGLAND AND WALES

There will, perhaps, be a fair number of people who feel critical of my decision to lump England and Wales, and the salmon beats thereof, into one chapter. If so, then all I can say is that I am sorry to have hurt their feelings. My purpose in writing this book, however, is not to simply list waters where salmon, however few they may be, are most convenient to those living in the South East England jungle! To be frank, there are rivers with far flung reputations which, if they were lifted from England and placed, say, between Spey and Dee, would hardly merit a mention. That is not to say, however, that good fishing does not exist outside Scotland in mainland Britain. Far from it indeed! In England, good salmon fishing is still to be enjoyed on its five principal producers: Hampshire Avon and the Dart in the southern half of the country, and the Tyne, Lune and Eden in the north. And in Wales there are the Conway, Dovey, Welsh Dee and, of course, the Wye. Let me start by taking a look at English waters. Tyne has now emerged from pollution to become the most productive of English salmon rivers, but as its salmon history is limited, its exclusion from detailed consideration will hopefully be excused.

HAMPSHIRE AVON

There are a number of rivers running under the name of Avon. In order to distinguish this one from the rest, it is known as the Hampshire Avon and yet, such is the way of such things, for most of its course it is flowing through Wiltshire! Rather than being known primarily as a salmon river, the Hampshire Avon has gained a reputation as a river for mixed fishing sport without equal in England. As a salmon fishery, it does not merit a great deal of attention in terms of sheer numbers. However, whatever this river's fish may lack in quantity, they more than make up for with their quality. How many rivers, anywhere, can boast early season salmon with an average weight in excess of 20lb? Quite marvellous fish. Every season, portmanteaux salmon, silver slabs of 30lb-plus springers are taken. Most of these leviathans fall to Devon minnows, fished slow and deep through the salmon's resting place. Fly is also fished, although not nearly so successfully. Remember, casting an upstream dry fly or nymph, which can work so well on the river's trout, is a very different proposition from heavy fly fishing for salmon, down and across, in thickly weeded water.

On that point, the Hampshire Avon is very much a chalkstream. Perhaps it is not in the classic mode of the Test and Itchen but, make no mistake, it is a chalkstream

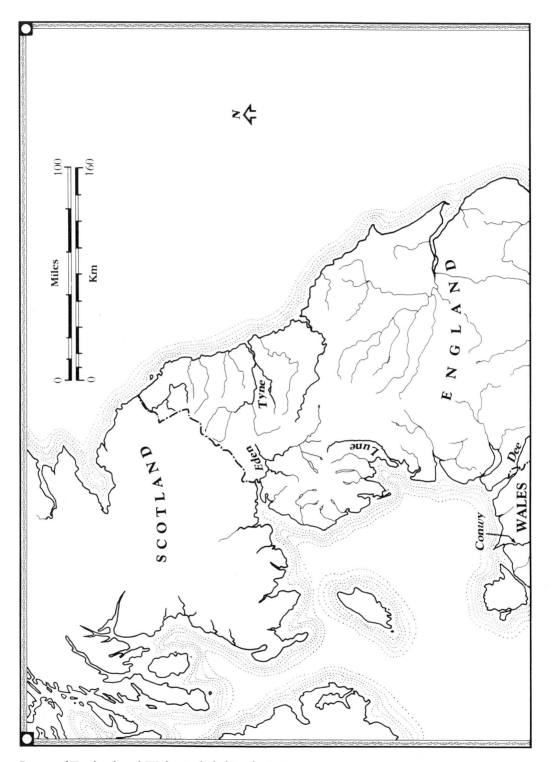

Rivers of England and Wales included in the test

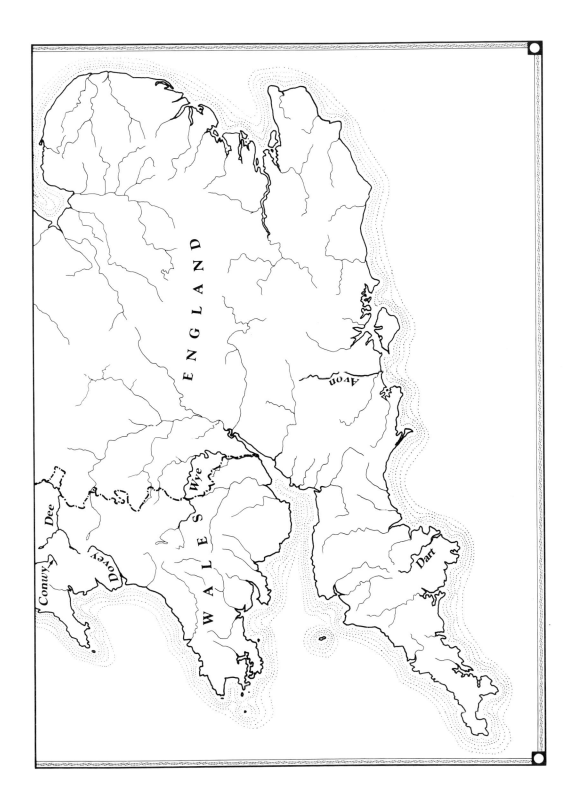

ENGLAND

WALES

Conwy

Dee

Dovey

Wye

Avon

Dart

Fishing the fly on the Hampshire Avon below Ibsley Bridge

A cock salmon of 46½lb from the Hampshire Avon's Bisterne Water, taken in May – the class of fish for which this river is justly famous all the same. Throughout its nearly fifty-mile length, the Avon passes majestically by bankside sedges bordering water meadows and lush pasturelands, in utter and complete contrast to the image of silvery salmon fighting their way up a Highland torrent.

Perhaps the best known fishery on the Hampshire Avon, so far as big spring salmon are concerned, is the Royalty Fishery at Christchurch. It was acquired by the West Hampshire Water Co in 1929 and, should its present capital value be realised, what an outstanding investment this will have proved to be. This fishery must also be practically unique in offering sea trout fishing from a punt!

Generally speaking, the best of this river's trout fishing lies above Salisbury, with its famous cathedral. This part of the river is widely known as the Upper Avon. At Salisbury, this upper river is joined by the Wylye, Nadder, Bourne and Ebble. It is obvious that the river is transformed from a character of relative intimacy into a substantial flow and, from here downstream, on what is known as the Lower Avon, the salmon fisheries are to be found: Britford, Trafalgar, the Bull Hotel's water at Downton, Burgate Manor and Charford, Breamore, Bickton Mill with seven miles of syndicated fishing, Ibsley North End, the very fine Somerley Fishery (perhaps best of all and stretching from above Ibsley Bridge down to Ringwood) and Ringwood itself, which produced the record Avon salmon of 51½lb. Another salmon of 49½lb was caught on neighbouring Several Fishery; then there are the Sopley Water, Avon Tyrrell and Winkton and Bisterne Fisheries before the Hampshire Avon flows through the Royalty Fishery and on to the sea at Christchurch.

THE DART

The Dart is widely recognised as having two principal sources, both set in the heart of one of England's last wilderness areas, the remotest part of northern Dartmoor. One source creates the East Dart, and the other gives birth to the West Dart. These two rivers join at Dartmeet and it is from here to the sea at Dartmouth, home of the Naval College, that the main river flows. As the name and setting implies, this is a swift, moorland river. It can also provide excellent sport with both salmon and sea trout, arguably the best in the West Country. The best salmon and sea trout fishing on the West Dart lies below Huccaby Bridge: the fishing on these upper stretches, owned and controlled by the Duchy of Cornwall, is strictly fly-only.

Salmon fishing on these upper rivers is heavily dependent on rainfall. This is true of any small, moorland spate stream. In a wet spring, salmon may be caught on the West Dart as early as April, although a May start is most typical. Sport usually peaks in August when, on the heels of a spate, excellent sport can be enjoyed with grilse and summer salmon. Incidentally, Dart salmon do not run particularly large, with an average weight in the region of 8lb.

On the main river, from Dartmeet down to Buckfast, some of the Dart's best salmon beats are to be found. Below Buckfastleigh and down to salt water virtually all the fishing is controlled by the Dart Anglers' Association. On these lower stretches salmon can be expected virtually from the opening of the season on 1 February, and this spring sport can be expected to peak in March and April, a time when salmon in the 20lb class can be expected, and a double-handed rod of about 13ft will take over from the more generally favoured approach to Dart salmon, made with a single-handed rod of about 9–10ft. This doubles for sea trout, for which the Dart has a justifiably high reputation.

THE LUNE

Leaping north from the West Country, the salmon fisherman may find little to interest him in England until he reaches the Lune, which enters the sea at Lancaster. The Lune still has a fine reputation, which it had a long and hard struggle to retain through the years of the scourge of UDN – Ulcerative Dermal Neucrosis – which left so many of our rivers as little more than stinking salmon mortuaries. Prior to the start of the disease at the end of the sixties, it had very substantial runs of spring salmon. Nowadays, the Lune is better known for summer and autumn sport with salmon.

Spinning at Avon Tyrrell on the Avon

The Lune is a spate river, and the quality of its fishing, in the short term, is very dependent upon rain falling on the Pennines and Cumbrian Fells. The best fishing time is limited. Following a mid-season spate, the high and dirty flood can be running off in a few short hours, when Lune regulars will be cancelling business appointments and dropping anything and everything, for the river will only give one or two days of good fishing conditions.

Salmon are rare in the upper reaches above Kirby Lonsdale much before September. This month and October can be good up there. Before that, grilse and late summer salmon seem reluctant to leave the lower river.

Much has been said and written about the Lune and its salmon. However, the simple fact of the matter is that, over recent times, the total catch for the entire river, taken from angler's returns, shows an average of little more than six hundred fish. While there are some very good salmon stretches such as the Halton Waters, and the Caton Beat of the Lancaster and District Angling Association, it always seems that whenever I speak to keen and loyal Lune fishermen it is sea trout, rather than salmon, to which the conversation almost inevitably turns.

THE EDEN

There is a temptation to include a number of Cumberland's salmon rivers, but it is perhaps best to concentrate on the Eden, jewel in the crown of North West England's salmon rivers.

The Eden has its source at a height of 2,328ft near High Seat on the Pennines, just three miles from the source of the Lune. From here, it flows a distance of some seventy miles before flowing out into the Solway Firth below Carlisle.

As on so many rivers, Eden talk tends to be of a glorious past, rather than the present. There was a time when it was rated second only to the Wye in terms of England and Wales. But then came UDN which played havoc with salmon runs on both the Scottish and English sides of the Solway. As a guide to the localised effect that this had, it was estimated that UDN caused an average drop of some 45 per cent in numbers of salmon returning to rivers but, on the Eden, returns fell by more than 70 per cent. Put another way, three quarters of this river's salmon were wiped out in a very short period and where there had been four salmon, now there was only one, ten where there had been forty. The dreadful disease seemed to bite hardest on spring running fish. Combined with the enormously increased inroads made by high seas and local netting, spring runs faded into total decline.

Up until the late sixties, the Eden was famed for its heavy runs of spring salmon. They were its principal attraction. I myself was raised on tales of the Eden's spring salmon fishing from my father, who spent many boyhood years living at Wetheral. It was a story of members of the Yorkshire Flyfishers' indulging in heavy spinning tactics to tempt the heavy silver springers. Perhaps they were hoping that their beat would produce a salmon to topple the 56-pounder from Warwick Hall Water off its record pedestal. Perhaps they were even hoping to better Miss Ballantine.

A lady angler on the Hampshire Avon's Somerley Water

Incidentally, the Warwick Hall salmon was caught in 1892 by George McKenzie fishing the Holm Gate Rocks and Warwick Hall continued to produce fish of close to this size right up to the start of UDN.

Last of the great Eden fish was a 45-pounder caught in 1965 by Hugh Fielding. After that disastrous time of 1966 and 1967, the total catch from the Eden fell from an annual average of almost 2,000 salmon to nearly five hundred. Unlike other Solway rivers, the Nith for example, which also suffered greatly but has steadily recovered to something like its former glory, the Eden never seems to have succeeded in re-establishing its salmon runs. The season of 1983 produced just 650 fish, and the following season this fell to 409. As an old friend of my father's summed it up, 'At best, all we can hope for compared to the old days is a poor season. Often as not, however, we end up with something that can only be described as b. awful.'

Where the Eden has also suffered, and in this way it is like other Solway rivers, is in the severe depletion not only of the numbers of its fish but in the fact that the pattern has changed from spring to autumn sport. One wonders what proportion of spring fish survived UDN. Sadly, it does not seem to have been enough, faced with intensive netting, for the re-establishment of the spring run. But it is not even as simple as that. The season of 1984 has been cited as a disastrous one on the Eden, with only 409 salmon shown on returns. And yet, the season had started off well. Eden anglers were saying the springers were back when January and February produced 160 salmon, and big ones among them. It may have been little more than a candle spluttering in the wind.

THE CONWAY

The Conway river, or Conwy as it is properly known, is a river that I have crossed many times, and yet never fished. I was at school on HMS Conway on Anglesey, but the river remains just a memory of glimpsed waters either going to or returning from away-matches. I have always felt this to be a great personal pity, for accounts of the Conway point to it being a real cracker of a sea trout river, and no slouch when it comes to producing sport with salmon. It is the principal salmon river in North Wales, draining the slopes of Snowdonia.

The Conway is a river that shows a great change in character. In its upper stretches, it is a wild, mountain stream; it then becomes a sedate, lowland flow, and all this happens in a relatively short distance. The Conway shows other character changes, too. It is an outstanding example of the nature of a spate river. After heavy rain, the Conway can readily overflow its banks, and worming is the favoured method to tempt salmon from sheltered areas. It is not too long before the river subsides, and out comes the spinning rod armed with a Toby or Mepps spoon. The Mepps can be deadly on smaller spate rivers. Next comes the time of the fly, although this is a method most associated with the lower part of the river, below the confluence with the tributary Llugwy, where the pools are more open. But the most popular method of taking salmon is perhaps the shrimp; it is certainly very widely used.

Besides the Conway, the other really fine game fishing river in this area of North Wales is the Dovey. If this had been a book on sea trout fishing, the Dovey would undoubtedly have merited a premier position. Both rivers are of similar size but the fact of the matter is that it is justifiable to regard the Dovey as a sea trout river with some salmon, while the Conway is rather a salmon river with some sea trout. It should be noted, on the other hand, that what Conway sea trout lack in numbers, ranging between 230 and 608 fish in the last ten seasons, their average weight is about 3lb and individual Conway sea trout can grow far larger. The Welsh sea trout record was set on the Conway in 1949 with a fish of 21½lb and, interestingly, the same season produced another sea trout of 21lb.

WELSH DEE

Just as the Aberdeenshire Dee is recognised as one of the finest Scottish salmon rivers, so the Welsh Dee is in the front rank of Welsh salmon rivers. It carries a number of classic salmon beats.

Perhaps the most productive beat on the Welsh Dee is the Junction Pool. This is found at the confluence of the Dee with the Alwen, a good river in its own right. Here, however, as on the whole of the river and due to a complex water supply system on the river's headwaters above Bala Lake, the fishing is subjected to compensation flows. It is found that the effect of this relatively stale water, when released, is to cause salmon to run upstream from the lower Dee more quickly than in former times. Beats in this Corwen, Berwyn area, and further down the mid-section, normally show their best in the months of mid and late summer. Toward Llangollen, the Midland Flyfishers have a syndicated beat which has produced more than sixty salmon in at least one recent season. Incidentally, Llangollen Weir, which once acted as a hindrance to salmon running the Dee, was dismantled back in the sixties. On this lower part of the river, spring and early summer are generally rated as the best time to make a visit to one of the local beats. Fly, shrimp and worm do well.

Jumping further downstream, past good beats like the Wynnstay Estate Water, and to below Erbiston, the river slows right down to stroll through the Cheshire Plain. There is a weir at Erbistock, which halts the ascent of spring salmon, acting as a temperature pool. It follows, obviously enough, that opening season fish are caught below this weir. Natural bait is banned at the start of the season, so the spun Devon minnow is the favoured lure.

The Welsh Dee may not yet be able to match its former glories but, with a reported catch of more than 700 salmon in 1986, it certainly augurs well for this river's future.

Looking to the history of the Welsh Dee is to see a scene of great days of salmon fishing. As on many Scottish salmon rivers, the growth of demand for salmon fishing is a fairly recent development, within the last half century. Before that, salmon were often plenty, but fishermen few. Salmon fishing was carried out, very largely, by the proprietor and his personal guests.

It is from these times that one of the oft told tales of salmon fishing arose. The man involved was Jack Spoor, the village blacksmith at Bangor-on-Dee. Having been told that there was a fine salmon resting in the Duke's Pool, only a few hundred yards from the site of his smithy below Bangor Bridge, Jack laid his hammer on the anvil, closed shop, and headed off with his rod. Now, Jack Spoor was something of a local legend when it came to tempting salmon. A small audience began to gather but try as Jack might with an assortment of flies, the salmon was having none of them. Perhaps Jack felt that he was losing face in front of his neighbours. He may have thought that if he sat down and ate his lunch they might lose interest and drift off when, perhaps, he might use some of his secret personal techniques when nobody was watching. However, at least one member of the audience did not go away. A small boy, watching Jack peel an orange, suggested that perhaps the salmon would favour a piece of fruit. To Jack's eternal credit, he humoured the lad, cutting off a sliver of peel and attaching it to the hook. You can probably guess the rest. The salmon weighed 17½lb.

Another great fisherman who cast a line over the waters of the Welsh Dee was Jack Hughes-Parry, often described as the Welsh salmon wizard. He was responsible for catching the river's record fish of 42lb. Like Jack Spoor, Jack Hughes-Parry was not above using odd lures for salmon. One of these creates a distinctly grisly fishing tale. Jack owned a sandy coloured female cat, which was obviously the centre of attraction for the local tom cats. Litter after litter were produced to the point where any more kittens had to be drowned at birth. He must have noticed the attractive way in which the wee souls' tails worked in the water. Jack Hughes-Parry cut off the tails, tied them onto a Devon minnow mount and proceeded to catch salmon with them on the Fechan beat at Llangollen. All this is described in his book *Fishing Fantasy*. It is said that his motto was 'Waste not, want not', but one cannot help wondering what his sandy cat and her kittens might have had to say on the matter. One hopes, at least, that she received some portion of the fish in return for her offspring having been 'sent to sea'.

THE WYE

In terms of the salmon rivers of England and Wales, most fishermen will agree that I have kept the very best till last. The Wye, the river that for part of its 150-mile course delineates the border between England and Wales, is largely regarded as the outstanding river in mainland Britain, outside of Scotland. And it is a river very much in the classic mould, with its succession of great holding pools and shallow, riffling streams. In much the same manner as the Hampshire Avon, the Wye and its best beats have a reputation as producers of big salmon. By big, I mean that salmon in the 40lb class are taken virtually each and every season.

The best ever Wye salmon was taken by Miss Doreen Davey in March 1923. What is it about unmarried ladies that attracts the larger salmon to their lures? Sadly,

The upper Wye at Erwood below Builth Wells

The Wye in August near Monmouth

Georgina Ballantine and, I suspect, Doreen Davey, are no longer with us to offer any sort of explanation that they might have. And remember, all you macho types out there, that not only are the British and Wye records held by the girls, but also the record salmon taken on fly – a salmon of 61lb caught by Mrs Morrison in the Wood o'Shaws pool of the River Deveron in Scotland. Incidentally, the Wye salmon caught by Doreen Davey weighed 59lb. You know, when considering the number of ladies who fish, a tiny minority compared to the vast majority made up of men, it is hard to believe that it was all a coincidence, and that Georgina, Doreen and Mrs Morrison were just lucky enough to be in the right place at the right time. The odds are just too heavily against them, and one cannot help but think that there must be something more to it. As a male, I draw little comfort from the fact that most of the country's leading chefs are men. Far better that we should catch those record salmon!

To return to the Wye, however, the favoured beats are such as the unexpectedly named Carrots, and others in the Fownhope, Whitney, Erwood and Ross area. It is certain that those beats between Hereford and Ross see the cream of the Wye's sport with salmon.

The mighty salmon of the opening months of the season have already been discussed. It is such salmon that the Wye is famous for producing. These fish will have entered the river as early as December, just after the spawning time, and will have a full ten or eleven months to wait before taking their turn on the redds. An average weight for these early spring salmon will be approaching 20lb. It is a rare event to catch a salmon that is not well into double figures in the months of February through to May. Scale readings show these early salmon to have spent three winters at sea, where rich feeding accounts for the heavy return weights, and then there will be a number of fish that have spent four winters sea feeding before their return; these are the big boys in the class, accounting for the 30-pounders and more.

At the tail end of this run, and overlapping with it, come salmon that have enjoyed just two winters at sea. If they arrive in March, they are known locally as 'small springers', with an average weight of about 10lb. If they delay their return until May, those couple of extra months mean that the average weight has increased to 12lb. These May and later running salmon are again known by a localised name which, in this case, is 'summers'.

Finally, the summer salmon are joined by grilse runs which can be expected in June. These smallest of salmon, having spent just one winter at sea, may weigh as little as 3lb, but can weigh as much as eight or nine, making them almost indistinguishable from the smaller class of summers. Grilse, as on most rivers, reach a peak in numbers running the river through July and August, and so the spread of single and multiple sea-winter grilse and salmon generation runs into the Wye is finally completed. I have, however, heard of a further run of grilse, very late in the season, arriving after the salmon fishing has come to an end either on 17 October or 25 October on that section of the river below Rhayader and on its tributaries. Presumably, the earlier close on the upper river is to avoid the disturbance and taking of spawning fish, or those on the verge, fish which in either case should be left unmolested.

As to techniques and tackles for fishing the Wye, thoughts turn immediately to the Devon minnow. This spinner accounts for most of the early season fish. The Toby is also very popular, as is natural bait. Some might choose not to approve, but the spinning prawn can work wonders on deep, slow stretches of the river. The 'garden fly', better known as a big worm, is also popular on a number of beats.

Fly fishing is generally kept in reserve for the arrival of the summers and grilse although, of course, there are Wye fishermen who fish fly, at least for part of the day, throughout the season. But for late spring and summer work, when the fly is more widely acknowledged, the usual floating line sizes from 4 down to 8 tied on doubles, trebles or tubes come to the fore. Popular patterns include what might be called the salmon fisherman's imitative patterns, like the Shrimp Fly, Usk Grub and General Practitioner, and more general patterns like the Blue Charm, Thunder and Lightning, Hairy Mary and Garry Dog.

The straight mile below Hay-on-Wye

Trying the fly at Hay-on-Wye

Catches on the Wye are heavily dependent on river conditions. Such are the vagaries of the British climate, therefore, that annual catches can fluctuate wildly. Rather than highlight the poor seasons, excuse me for concentrating on the best in the last half century. Surprisingly, perhaps, the majority of these occurred in the sixties and on into the seventies: 1966: 6,991; 1967: 7,864; 1972: 7,433; 1973: 5,542; 1974: 5,758; and 1975: 6,796.

Besides the effect of the climate on annual catches as a whole it also affects, on a shorter term basis, how well the river fishes and which sections of it are likely to produce the heaviest catches. Of course, this is true on many rivers, particularly long ones such as the Wye. Remember, there are 150 miles between headwaters and estuary. The Wye has a big catchment area and is noted for experiencing enormous spates following prolonged rain. Equally, rain can be localised and may effect only one of the Wye's fairly large number of substantial tributaries. For example, localised rain on the headwaters of the Lugg will bring this river into spate but, upstream of its confluence with the Wye, the main river remains low and stale. The effect of this fresh, oxygenated water flowing into the main river is that beats below the Lugg can find themselves enjoying good sport with the stirred fish while, just upstream of the junction, the salmon remain comatosed.

The normal pattern, however, is for a general spate affecting the entire catchment area, when the Wye and all its tributaries can be expected to come into spate at roughly the same time. Water levels are vitally important to salmon fishing prospects on any river. The fresh water of a spate stirs resident fish and brings new fish into a beat, both classes being most likely to fall to the temptation of bait, spinner or fly as the water falls and clears. What happens on the Wye is that the headwaters clear first, while the lower river remains high and dirty. This state of affairs can last for a few days and, while it does, the best sport will obviously be enjoyed on the upper river.

Another notable effect of the great length of the Wye is simply that salmon take a long time to reach the upper river. January and February can see sport on lower beats, while upper beats normally have to wait until March. These upper beats in the section between Hay-on-Wye and Builth Wells will continue to fish well, in a normal season, until June. Sport dies away in the following months. Then comes late September and October and upper beat rods are active again, harvesting the grilse.

ACKNOWLEDGEMENTS

I hope that the enormous number of people who have so kindly helped with information to aid the preparation of this book will forgive me for not mentioning them all – the list would fill pages of this book. But let me assure you that my thoughts and thanks are with you.

I will, however, single out three names: Bill Currie, that great Scottish salmon fisherman and writer, who provided photographs, as did Mike Shepley – and an especially big thankyou to Mrs P. M. Tarlton for providing so many wonderful photographs taken by her late husband, John Tarlton.

Many, many thanks to you all.

INDEX